'Jewish Gandhi' of Cochin

Abraham Barak Salem - A
20th Century Nationalist/Zionist
& His Cochin Assembly Speeches

'Jewish Gandhi'
OF Cochin

A Biography Of Abraham Barak Salem
- A 20th Century Nationalist/Zionist
& His Cochin Assembly Speeches

Bala Menon
Dr. Essie Sassoon

TAMARIND TREE
Toronto

Other books published by Tamarind Tree
as part of its *Cochin Jewish Catalogue:*

1. *Spice & Kosher: Exotic Cuisine of the Cochin Jews*
   by Dr. Essie Sassoon, Bala Menon and Kenny Salem

2. *Order of Mourning in Cochin Jewish Tradition*
   by Shlomo Mordechai

'Jewish Gandhi' OF Cochin

A Biography Of Abraham Barak Salem
- A 20th Century Nationalist/Zionist
& His Cochin Assembly Speeches

Bala Menon
Dr. Essie Sassoon

TAMARIND TREE
Toronto

Tamarind Tree Books Inc.,
14 Ferncastle Crescent,
Brampton, Ontario. L7A 3P2, Canada.
or email: ttb.imprint@gmail.com

Library and Archives Canada Cataloguing in Publication

Title: 'Jewish Gandhi' of Cochin : Abraham Barak Salem - a 20th century nationalist/Zionist / Bala Menon, Dr. Essie Sassoon.
Names: Menon, Bala, - author. | Sassoon, Essie, - author.
Description: Includes bibliographical references.
Identifiers: Canadiana 2020030853X | ISBN 9780993819933 (softcover)
Subjects: LCSH: Salem, A. B. | LCSH: Jews—India—Cochin (Princely State) — Biography. | LCSH: Nationalists—India—Cochin (Princely State) — Biography. | LCSH: Zionists—India—Cochin (Princely State)—Biography. | LCSH: Statesmen—India—Cochin (Princely State)—Biography. | LCSH: Social reformers—India—Cochin (Princely State)—Biography. | LCGFT: Biographies.

Classification: LCC DS135.I63 S356 2020 | DDC 954/.83—dc23

Cover picture of A. B. Salem inside the Paradesi Synagogue: Helen Sirkin (1965).
Back cover picture of the interior of the Paradesi Synagogue: Bala Menon (2012).

This book is dedicated to the
descendants of
Abraham Barak Salem
in India, Israel, Canada,
the United Kingdom & Australia

Other books published by Tamarind Tree
as part of its *Cochin Jewish Catalogue:*

1. *Spice & Kosher: Exotic Cuisine of the Cochin Jews*
   by Dr. Essie Sassoon, Bala Menon and Kenny Salem

2. *Order of Mourning in Cochin Jewish Tradition*
   by Shlomo Mordechai

Contents

FOREWORD

A. B. Salem was fully Jewish and fully Indian. He was a religious Jew and pioneering Zionist as well as an ardent transformational local and nationalist political figure as documented in his Cochin Assembly speeches. This "Jewish Gandhi" is most deserving of the meticulous rendering of his story by Bala Menon and Dr. Essie Sassoon. This biography furthers Menon's efforts in his blog (*jewsofcochin.blogspot.com*) to recover and preserve the full factual history of Kerala's Jews.

It is very important for the world to learn that Kerala has been a place where Jews have been welcomed to be Jews and full members of society.

For example, Menasseh ben Israel cited the Raja of Cochin's full acceptance of and favoritism toward Jews in his appeal to Oliver Cromwell to allow Jewish settlement in England.

The Paradesi Synagogue is a tourist attraction as a symbol of that relationship. As Salem put it, visitors would see "the life of the Bible" on a "street that was built religiously and not as a ghetto". Today, Chennamangalam where the palace of the Paliam family is surrounded by a synagogue, mosque, church, and Hindu temple, is being promoted as another example of a long history of tolerance and acceptance. What another place in the world can claim that Jewish life there was not shaped by endemic anti-Semitism?

Menon and Sassoon also recount the disturbing history of the social structure of the Jewish communities of Kerala, where the Paradesi (foreign) Jews enforced a system that did not accept the "religious purity" and ancestry of most of the other Jews.

This entire system was clearly against Jewish law according to outside rabbinical authorities from the sixteenth century on, but the Paradesi Jews refused to recognize most Jews as equals with full ritual and entry rights in their synagogue.

Salem used Gandhian methods of protest to change all that. He fasted and led his family in sit-down strikes in the synagogue. Menon and Sassoon clearly place Salem's approach within the general problem of restricted Hindu temple entry in Kerala, Travancore's proclamations on temple entry, and Gandhian responses such as the Trichur Temple Entry Satyagraha Committee.

Menon and Sassoon give the full history of Salem's struggles back to its beginnings with the romantic relationship between A. B. Salem's great-grandparents, a leader of the Paradesi Jewish community and a manumitted slave through the salacious tales told about the A. B Salem's family to thwart his efforts.

Even before he gained full ritual rights, Salem had long been a business partner of wealthy Jewish leader and entrepreneur S. S. Koder and had written a guidebook to the synagogue. Ironically, Koder was also his chief antagonist in synagogue affairs. Salem's victory is reflected in a 1968 painting in the Paradesi Synagogue where Salem is depicted with Koder as an honoured member rather than an outsider excluded from entering the synagogue.

Dr. Kenneth Robbins
Washington D.C. / 2020

INTRODUCTION

Babu Nechemia's eyes welled up when he whispered the words "Salem Mutha" or Grandfather Salem.

We had travelled by car from Ashkelon on the Mediterranean coast and were at the fortified gates of Moshav Nevatim in the Negev desert of southern Israel. Babu was a short, stocky man, a machine gun slung across his shoulder and we could see other weapons in racks in the guardhouse behind him.

Kenny Salem introduced us in Hebrew as visitors from Cochin and Babu's demeanour changed instantly. He was all smiles, and when he heard that Kenny was Avraham Barak's *perakutty* (grand-child in Malayalam, the language of the southern Indian state of Keala), he was very welcoming. A gush of conversation followed, about how his family and others in the settlement owed their life in Israel to Salem Mutha.

His own parents had come to Israel in the early 1950s because of A. B. Salem's direct political intervention on behalf of hundreds of Cochin Jews stranded in Bombay and Ernakulam after they embarked on their *aliyah*. (*Aliyah* is Hebrew for 'ascent' or the movement of Jews from the diaspora to the Holy Land. *Aliyah* also refers to being called up for the reading of the Torah in the synagogue).

We later met Yitzakh Nehemia, Shalom, Miriam, Yasmin and many others in Moshav Nevatim who all paid tributes to Salem's

efforts and his friendship with Israeli leaders that helped the Cochin Jews return to their fatherland. There are more than 600 happy Cochin Jews in Nevatim today, whose hearts continue to beat
for Kerala. Most work on their own farms and many are employed
in the industrial towns of Beersheba and Dimona.

Later, at Moshav Taoz, midway between Tel Aviv and Jerusalem,
community leader Yosef Oren, who was part of the Kadavumbhagam Congregation in Kerala, told us of the travails in Ernakulam
in 1953 after scores of families had sold all their belonging to go to
Israel. "We stayed on the beaches with a tarpaulin over our heads;
our parents bought and sold fish, waiting for the call from Jerusalem. And it was Salem Mutha who answered our prayers." (See the
Aliyah story and the Salem connection in Chapter 8. Salem, Zionism & The *Aliyah*: Page 144.)

None of these Cochin Jews belonged to Salem's congregation.
They were all members of the so-called Black Jews of Malabar who
made *aliyah* because of the Messianic zeal with which they embraced Zionism and the birth of Israel. Salem was, however, the *de
facto* leader of the Cochin Jews because of his intellect, erudition,
political clout and his passion to fight for the underprivileged.

Salem belonged to a small community called Brown Jews by
Western scholars and derided as '*meshuchrarim*' or manumitted
slaves by other Jews who were at the top of the religious and social rung in Jewish Cochin. The *meshuchrarim* were also referred to
as *ulmakkar* (people accepted into the fold) by the Paradesi community of White Jews and were discriminated against, although
economically most were quite well off. While there was often close
interaction in social, cultural and economic life, animosity was
overt within the synagogue and in religious affairs.

On the other hand, there were no social or cultural interactions
between the Black Jews and the Paradesis from the 16th century,
with the Brown Jews siding with the Paradesis. The social structure reflected the caste-ridden Hindu society of Cochin at the
time, and prejudice was undisguised and often brutal.

From the late 19th century, however, the Brown Jews began
revolting against their treatment in the synagogue and their clas-
sification as 'freed slaves'. The Brown Jews were not allowed to say

certain prayers, were made to sit on the floor of the synagogue, prohibited from marrying members of the White Jews and not allowed to bury their dead in the Paradesi cemetery or in coffins.

It was Salem's grandfather, Avraham or Avo, who started the rebellion which continued until the mid-20th century, when Salem, following Gandhian methods of protest, succeeded in shattering the illegal, anti-Jewish system and brought equality into the synagogue. Social stratification in Mattancherry began to end gradually in the 1930s with the community becoming more cohesive over the years until most of them left to settle in Israel.

•••••

A BRIEF HISTORY (*Excerpted from the blog: jewsofcochin.ca*).

The Cochinim or the Cochin Jews of the southwestern Indian state of Kerala comprises one of the tiniest and most ancient of all Jewish communities in the Diaspora. They trace their history on the Malabar coast to 2,000 years ago, first landing on those pristine, rain-swept shores as sailors in the fleets of King Solomon to purchase spices, apes, peacocks and precious metals.

Songs and oral traditions of this community give us a glimpse of their early settlements in Malabar in places like Paloor, Madai and the port of Cranganore (today's Kodungalloor), soon after the destruction of the Second Temple in 70 CE. They call this the 'First Diaspora'.

One of the stories suggests they are descendants of Jews taken captive by Nebuchadnezzar in the 6th century BCE and came to India after being freed by the Persian king Cyrus the Great.

The community has almost disappeared today, with only a few left in Kerala state. There are no services or prayers, although the magnificent 452-year-old Paradesi Synagogue in Mattancherry is still open and functional during festival days when Israeli tourists gather or when a Chabad Rabbi visits from Mumbai.

Recorded history shows that Jews were present in Kerala in 849 CE. Hebrew names were engraved on copper plates granted by a Kerala Hindu king Ayyan Adikal Thiruvadikal of Venad (near modern-day Kollam or old Quilon) to Syrian Christian settlers, who were part of a trade guild called Manigramam and led by one Mar

Sapir Iso. Jews signed these Tharissapalli plates as witnesses, along with others who signed in the Pahlavi and Kufic languages. The plates were given on behalf of Chera ruler Sthanu Ravi Varman.[1]

In 1000 CE, legendary Kerala emperor Cheraman Perumal Kulashekhara Bhaskara Ravi Varman, from his palace at Mahodayapuram in the Cranganore area, issued two copper plates to a Jewish merchant Issappu Irrappan (Joseph Rabban), believed to be of Yemeni descent. The plates conferred on the Jewish community 72 proprietary rights equivalent to those held by the Nairs, the then martial nobles of Malabar.[2]

This was during the 100-year war between the Kerala Cheras and the Imperial Cholas of the Tamil kingdom and it is believed that the Jewish community contributed men and material (especially naval forces) to help the Chera emperor in the war effort.[3]

The copper plate inscriptions mention that several land rights and other honours were being given to the Jews in perpetuity "as long as the earth and the moon remain". Rabban was also made chief of a powerful trade guild called Anjuvannam, that many early Western writers believed to be a princely state. Thus began the privileged existence of the Jews in Kerala. For almost five centuries, they thrived in their major settlement of Cranganore as traders and artisans before the community moved to Cochin after cataclysmic floods in the River Periyar and attacks by Muslims.

The copper plates are preserved in the Paradesi Synagogue. Replicas of these plates were presented to a delighted then-Israeli Prime Minister Shimon Peres on September 09, 1992, when he visited India - a heart-warming piece of evidence that there was a safe haven for Jews in this little corner of India, centuries before the dream of Israel became a reality.[4]

Israeli president Ezer Weizman visited the synagogue in January 1997, hailing Cochin as a "symbol of the persistence of Judaism

---

1 Aiyya, V. N. Nagom. *Travancore State Manual*, pg 244.

2 Menon, A. Sreedhara. *A Survey of Kerala History*, DC Books, Kottayam, 2008, pg 45.

3 Narayanan, M.G.S. *Cultural Symbiosis in Kerala*, Kerala Historical Society, Trivandrum, 1972, pg 34.

4 The Hindu, *http://www.hindu.com/2003/09/11stories/2003091108060400.htm*

and of *aliyah* ... I pay tribute to India for taking care of the Jews and their places of worship ..."[5]

By the 17th century, there were 11 congregations with their own synagogues – three in Mattancherry (Kadavumbhagam, Thekkumbhagam and Paradesi), two in Ernakulam (Kadavumbhagam and Thekkumbhagam - yes, same names!), one each in Chennamangalam, Mala, Paloor, Muttam and Tirutur, and a splendid one in Paravur (at that time under the control of the King of Travancore). Cochin Jewish songs also tell of a synagogue in a place called Southi (this place has not yet been identified!).

It is of interest to note here that in the late 18th century, Cochin was more important to the Jews than New York. Walter Fischel, a scholar of Oriental Jewry, wrote: "Cochin, one of the oldest Jewish settlements on Asian soil, had a much larger Jewish community than New York and surpassed it not only numerically, but also culturally. The Cochin Jewish community in 1792 had about 2,000 Jews ... and 9 synagogues of considerable antiquity, while New York had only 72 Jewish families and only one synagogue."[6]

•••••

We owe a lot to Dr. Nathan Katz (considered the Dean of Indo-Judaic studies) and Ellen Goldberg, whose voluminous research on the Cochin Jews provided leads in preparing this biography.

Dr. Barbara Johnson and Ruby Daniel's book *Ruby of Cochin* offers glimpses into A. B. Salem's life in Jew Town and of his grandfather Avo. Thanks to Dr. Johnson for allowing us to cite from the book.

Dr. Kenneth Robbins is a psychiatrist and collector of South Asian art. He has edited two books: *Western Jews in India: From the Fifteenth Century to the Present* and *Jews and the Indian National Art Project*. We acknowledge the help of Dr. Robbins in the completion of this book.

A. B. Salem's third son Gumliel Salem, who lived in Jew Town, Mattancherry, and who died in February 2016, contributed a lot

---

5 From video of Weizman's visit to Paradesi Synagogue. In possession of Bala Menon.

6 Fischel, Walter. *From Cochin, India, to New York*, pp. 265-67, cited by Katz in *Last Jews of Cochin*, pg 102. *Harry Austrynn Wolfson Jubilee Volume*. Jerusalem: American Academy for Jewish Research, pp 255-75.

to this biography, speaking for hours about his well-known father and for arranging to get his speeches. His wife, the late Reema Salem (who passed away in August, 2015) also provided insights into Salem's life.

We are grateful to Prof. James Chiriyankandath who was the first to write a paper devoted to A. B. Salem - *Nationalism, religion and community: A. B. Salem, the politics of identity and the disappearance of Cochin Jewry*, which we have sourced for information about Salem's early political life.

Thanks to Rema Menon for proofreading the manuscript.

We also wish to thank A. B. Salem's grandchildren in India, Israel and Canada for all the little bits of information that went into fleshing out the story of Salem.

They include:
Dr. Usha Mohan, Hubli, Karnataka, India,
Mathew Antony, Ernakulam, Kerala, India,
Dr. Leslie & Dr. Glennis Salem, Haifa, Israel,
Dr. Cynthia and Dr. Muralee Dharan, Tiberias, Israel,
Linda and Steve Hertzman, Vancouver, Canada,
Kenny Salem, Toronto, Canada.

And others:
Rohan Sabharwal, Filmmaker, Mumbai, Maharashtra, India,
Dr. Ophira Gamliel, Jerusalem, Israel,
Susannah Sirkin, New York, United States,
Pearly Simon, Haifa, Israel,
Prem Doss Yehudi, Trivandrum, Kerala, India,
Ravi Kuttikad, Ernakulam, Kerala, India,
Abraham David, Tiberias, Israel,
Several Cochini Jews in Moshav Nevatim, Moshav Taoz and Petat Tikvah.

Bala Menon
Toronto / September, 2020

CHAPTER I

The 'Salem Maidan'

Avraham Baruch Salem was a small man in a corner of a large ground. However, he was standing atop a grassy knoll in a corner and had a good view of the ground. He began gesticulating and calling out to some labourers squatting in groups and discussing their workdays before heading to the nearest toddy shops and their homes. "*Varu, varoo* (Come, come in Malayalam)," Salem shouted. Some of them got up, looked at each other, and walked towards Salem. Most of them worked in the docks and small machining shops in the area or were rickshaw-pullers.

A few minutes earlier, they had seen the sprightly Salem leap from a *jhowka* (a horse-drawn carriage), after riding into the ground from somewhere around the boat jetty that could be seen from where he stood. Beyond was the brilliant blue of the Arabian Sea, the rippling shadows of the waves darkening under the evening light.

Salem launched into a tirade of how the Cochin administration was being unkind to workers in the Kingdom and about the need for them to organize for political and social activism in the tightly-structured, hierarchical society.

The year was 1926. The Russian Revolution had created a stir among the working classes of the world; the First World War had ended with ideas of emancipation and freedom taking roots in British India; the Jallianwala Bagh massacre of 1919[1] had given impetus to the Indian nationalist movement and the trio of Mohandas Gandhi, Gopalakrishna Gokhale and Bal Gangadhar Tilak was charting out a road plan for Indian independence.

The nominally independent Cochin Kingdom (the British exercised political control through an appointed Diwan or administrator) had taken the progressive step of establishing a Legislative Council in 1925 of which Salem was a founding-member. Salem's early speeches in the *maidan* reflected his far-sighted interventions in the assembly.

Retired journalist and Ernakulam resident Ravi Kuttikad remembers stories told by his seniors about A. B. Salem.

"Salem was an idiosyncratic personality. He used to come in a horse-driven carriage *(tonga* or *jhowka)* some evenings and stand on the sandy mount[2] at the far end of the ground that is today called Rajendra Maidan (just off Park Avenue in the Pallimukku area of Ernakulam.)"[3]

Surrounding the ground were the homes of prominent Nair families of the time, many of them related to the Paliath Achans of Chennamangalam. (The Paliath Achans were the hereditary prime ministers of Cochin, before the British began exerting political hegemony over the Kingdom. During the Second World War, several British Army officers stayed in many of the Paliath houses in the area. The Nairs were the traditional warriors of Kerala, forming the bulk of the military and security forces of the Cochin Maharaja.)

Kuttikad says that people in the neighbourhood talked about this Jew's 'abnormal behaviour'. In the dim light of dusk, Salem harangued the dozen or so labourers, hawkers and boat workers who gathered there to rest and chat. Some passersby also stopped to listen. Most of them were drunk. "There were also many *'nado-*

---

1 The Jallianwala Bagh massacre took place on 13 April, 1919, when Brigadier-General Reginald Dyer ordered British troops to fire into a crowd of unarmed Indian civilians in Jallianwala Bagh, Amritsar, Punjab, killing 379 people and injuring over 1,200.

2 The sandy mount was later levelled and made into a small wooden platform.

3 Kuttikad, Ravi. Personal communication, February 2015.

dis' camping in different parts of the ground, who turned up to listen to Salem." (*Nadodis* are gypsies, wandering minstrels and street performers, who were always blamed for petty crimes by local officials.)

Salem's thundering speeches were about "how Mattancherry's development was being ignored by the administration and also about the economic and social disparities within the Cochin population," recounts Kuttikad. "On some days, there were hardly two or three people on the ground, but Salem would go on and on about society's ills and problems."

Salem spoke mostly in English, interspersed with Malayalam words, and his listeners obviously didn't understand a word of it or the significance of his theories, although it is said they laughed and clapped animatedly whenever Salem raised a hand or pointed to the horizon.

Later, when he got more involved with labour unions and organizational work, he used Malayalam at the grassroots level to fire up his listeners, who now included workers in coir, cashew, coconut and vegetable oil processing units, brick kilns, fisheries and dock labourers.

After some time, the platform or the mound of sand on which he stood came to be known as Salem *Kunnu* (*kunnu* is 'hill' in Malayalam) and when Salem gained prominence in local politics as a distinguished member of the Cochin Legislative Council, the ground itself was named Salem Maidan.

Writer T. C. Narayan, who lives in Bengaluru in the neighbouring state of Karnataka, remembers A. B. Salem as having been a frequent visitor to his grandfather's house in Ernakulam. "I recall references to his (Salem's) mischievous sense of humour and acerbic tongue," Narayan writes in his book *Ettukettu Stories* which has three pages devoted to Salem.

Narayan confirms the story of the 'Salem Mound', which he describes as a 'small platform with a few steps leading up to it.'

Salem, according to Narayan, was always impeccably dressed in a suit and wearing his traditional skullcap.

"He had a flowing beard and spoke passionately...and there was much heckling and banter when he spoke, but he did succeed in creating some public awareness regarding local issues."[4]

A two-boat jetty in front of the ground was called Huzoor Jetty, which was used by members of the Royal Family when they came to Cochin from the main palace at Thrippunithura.[5] At the southern end of the Huzoor Jetty is a statue of Maharaja Sri Rama Varma, unveiled by then Viceroy of India Lord Linlithgow on January 8, 1939. (*Sir Sri Rama Varma XVI GCIE {1858 – March 21, 1932} was the ruler of Cochin from 1915 to 1932.*)

Historian V. N. Venugopal has also talked about Salem and this historic ground. "What is today's Foreshore Road was an expanse of grey waters... Large swathes of land in the area... belonged to the family of the Paliath Achan. In front of the Huzoor Jetty, there was a platform, which was called the Salem Mount, where Salem, a prominent Jew of Cochin... used to sit and give speeches against the government."[6]

The Huzoor Kacheri or the Secretariat of the Cochin Government was later built at one end of the ground.

The *maidan*, often compared with London's Hyde Park, retained the name Salem Maidan until March 6, 1947, when the then president of the Indian National Congress Acharya Kripalani[7] renamed it as Rajendra Maidan - after Rajendra Prasad who became the first President of independent India.

Kripalani made the announcement during a public speech, after getting a message to this effect from the Maharaja. By this time, Salem was no longer a force in local politics and a new generation of radical political leaders didn't even know there was such a man living in Mattancherry.

The Maidan was the venue of huge rallies addressed by Indian nationalists like Mahatma Gandhi, Annie Besant, Jawaharlal

---

4 Narayan T. C. *Ettukettu Stories*, Unison Publications, Bangalore, 2007, pg 116.

5 Thripunithura was the capital of the Kingdom of Cochin. Today, it is part of Ernakulam district and of the Kochi Metropolitan area.

6 Menon, Anasuya. 'Pasts converge, history unfurls', *The Hindu*, September 26, 2013.

7 The Indian National Congress was founded in 1885 and spearheaded the Indian freedom movement. Acharya J. B. Kripalani was secretary of the Congress Party from 1934 to 1945 and then party president at the time of Indian Independence. He was succeeded to the top party post by Rajendra Prasad.

Nehru, Nobel-laureate Rabindranath Tagore and E. M. S. Namboodiripad, the firebrand leader who led the first democratically elected Communist government in the world in 1957. It was also the venue for pitched battles between freedom fighters and the authorities in the years before independence.

(Some Cochini Jews say that Salem Kunnu was inside Irvin Park - today's Subash Chandra Bose Park near Rajendra Maidan. Salem's third son the late Gumliel Salem said he also thought the mount was inside Irvin Park, opposite the Ernakulathappan Shiva Temple in the same area.")[8]

By 1957, many of the ideals that Salem preached on social justice had disappeared from day to day dialogue. Class war was out in the open and power had shifted from the intellectual class to the rabble-rousers. Class had become crass and Salem withdrew into himself, content with his synagogue, family and grandchildren until his death ten years later in Jew Town.

Today, few in Kerala know or have heard of Salem Kunnu and Salem Maidan; even people in Mattancherry know little of the man for whom a small road connecting Jew Town Road and Maulana Azad Road was named.

Most auto-rickshaw drivers and shoppers in the area refer to A. B. Salem Road with the Muslim name of Abu Salim or Abu Saleem Road! The municipal road sign is spelt 'A. B. Selam'. The late journalist T. V. R. Shenoy wrote in 2008: "...It is an easy enough mistake to make I suppose, but it is completely incorrect. Being a fellow Kochi man is one of the reasons I knew about A. B. Salem..."[9]

There is a small shelter and a resting place for labourers and head-load workers - named informally after Salem - in the next street, and managed by the local unit of Center of Indian Trade Unions (CITU), the militant labour wing of the Communist Party of India (Marxist), which today runs the Kerala Government.

---

8 Gumliel Salem passed away in Mattancherry in 2017. Personal communication.

9 Shenoy, T. V. R. *The Jewish Gandhi and Barack Obama*, Rediff, September 8, 2008.

CHAPTER II

A Grandson Remembers

Leslie Abraham Salem is the eldest of A. B. Salem's grandchildren, son of Balfour and Seema (Koder) Salem. Here, he talks about his grandfather 'Daddypapa' in a letter to the authors.

Leslie Salem,[1]
Haifa, Israel.

Abraham Barak Salem was my paternal grandfather and my Jewish name of Abraham was taken from my grandfather's name, this being the traditional Jewish custom.

My sister (Cynthia) was named Ruth (her Jewish name) after my paternal grandmother. My father Ebenezer Balfour Salem was the fourth child of my grandparents and he was an engineer by profession. He studied at the Maharaja's College in Ernakulam and took a Bachelor's degree in Mathematics.

He further continued his studies at the Guindy Engineering College in Madras from where he obtained his Bachelor's degree in Engineering. He was employed at the government institution of All India Radio (also known as AIR or Aakashvani and now called

---

1 Dr. Leslie Salem is a Professor at Technion in Haifa, one of Israel's premier universities.

Doordarshan) and was posted at several different places in India such as Madras (today's Chennai), Trivandrum, Bangalore and New Delhi.

In the early 20th century, as a young lawyer, my grandfather spent considerable energy in setting right some discrimination that existed among the Jews that lived in Jew Town.

My grandfather was considered as belonging to a section of the Jews that were manumitted and hence did not receive the full rights of religious practice in the Paradesi Synagogue where he attended. After prolonged protests and persistence on his part, these wrongs were righted and during my childhood days it was non-existent.

My father (Balfour) married my mother Seema (Baby) Koder who belonged to the Paradesi community and this caused quite an uproar in the community. They finally came to terms with it and in my childhood days, as far as I can remember, there were no signs of any discrimination in the synagogue.

A few years later, my uncle Gumliel married Reema, a member of the Paradesi community, but this time there was hardly any uproar. My childhood days were spent in Jew Town and have only good memories of them. My father was posted out of Cochin State most of the time and my mother and sister and myself lived in our family house in Jew Town (Mattancherry).

Our house was a big one, having two storeys. We all lived on the upper floor and my grandfather also had a bedroom on the lower floor, which was more convenient for him.

I remember he had a big oval table, which he called 'My Office Table' on which he used to work occasionally. This table was in the drawing room of the upper floor and was quite a luxurious piece of furniture with green matting in the centre (of the type we find today atop a billiard table) .

It also served as a massive dining table during the extended family gatherings at the Passover Festival, which generally falls in March or April. My grandfather was very particular on celebrating the Passover festival with all the family – especially inviting my Aunt Malka, Uncle Antony and cousins Mathew and Rosy, to the table. Aunt Malka and family stayed in Ernakulam whereas my other aunt Venetia and family were put up in Hubli (in the neighbouring state of Karnataka). Also, he made it a point to have the Pascal lamb at the table as mentioned in the Bible.

(Salem himself described the Feast of Passover ritual in his booklet *'Eternal Light - The Cochin Jew Town Synagogue'* - *"Every Jewish child is made to feel the glow of Freedom gained in Egypt by the forefathers and the story of the Redemption is vividly and impressibly repeated with ceremony and chanting... round the family table with goblets of wine in front of them to make their hearts merry as they proceed to narrate the great events of the breaking of the fetters of the bondage and the going out of our forefathers from Egypt."*[2]

Salem wrote about the festive dinner of 1920s Jew Town (and which continued well into the 1960's): "A lad, with a knapsack on his back "runs round the table with a staff in hand to symbolize the hasty journey out of Egypt and the eating of bitter herbs and the unleavened cakes made out ground kosher wheat... and the drinking of the wine in joy and the deliverance... and the Festival table service ends with the hope repeated throughout the centuries of dispersion 'May the next year see us in Jerusalem".)

My grandfather always ensured that the table was laden with the choicest fruits, especially the season's best variety of mangoes such as *Malgova, Kudadas, Alphonso, Priur* etc and other fruits such as pineapples, sapotas[3] and jackfruit etc.

He used to have his daily dinner in the evening with a 'Thali' (plate) with seven to eight selected items, one of which was some gold powder mixed with honey. He had a problem with diabetes but couldn't care less about it as far as his meals were concerned.

He used to pray daily in the morning in the house and at the synagogue on the Jewish Shabbat which starts on a Friday evenings and ends on Saturday evening.

It goes without saying that all the festivals and fasts were strict-

---

2 Salem, A.B. *Eternal Light, Cochin Jew Town Synagogue,* Ernakulam, 1929, pg 36.

3 Sapota - also known as sapodilla or chikoo.

ly adhered to. He was a staunch Jew and proud of it. As far as I can remember he always had a cap (the *kippah*) on his head wherever he went. Usually, this is a sign of a religious Jewish person.

The festival of Simchat Torah is the last in a series of festive celebrations and is celebrated every year by Jews all over the world. In Jew Town, it was a special custom to mark the end of the festival by walking along the street of Jew Town, starting from the synagogue gate and stopping at the doorsteps of some of the elders in the community to get their blessings.

My grandfather's house was one of the stops and it was a custom initiated by him to distribute some small eats and ice-cream cones to the community crowd. As children, we always looked forward to this treat.

(Ruby Daniel has also mentioned this as happening in earlier years: A. B. Salem held a party for the whole community in the evening of the second day of Simchat Torah. Ruby wrote that everyone on Jew Street held 'Open House' on that day, with abundant food and drinks on the dining tables. No invitation was necessary. Drink flows like water[4] and it was Salem's house that was the first stop for all men to kick off the party.)

Towards the last years of his life he had trouble with reading, because of his failing eyesight. It was my privilege and duty to read the daily newspaper headlines to him for which he gave me some money to spend or save as I chose.

I collected these coins and occasionally used them to rent a bicycle which as a kid I used to enjoy very much riding on. Another of my duties was to take him to the synagogue for prayers if I was around at that time. Since he couldn't walk freely at his age we had a wheel-chair permanently at home for his use.

I used to push the wheelchair rather fast and my grandfather, while seated in the chair, used to clear the way with his walking stick swinging left and right so as to make sure we didn't bang into anything on the way. He seemed to enjoy the speed of the wheel-

---

4 Daniel Ruby & Johnson Barbara C. *Ruby of Cochin: An Indian Jewish Woman Remembers*, Jewish Publication Society, Philadelphia, 1995, pg 173.

chair though I used to get lectured down by others saying that it was dangerous and not the right thing to do.

Unfortunately, I didn't realize the capacity and drive of my grandfather while he was still alive. It was much later, that I become more acquainted with his work and activities, especially in helping the *Aliyah* to Israel of the Malabari Jewish community.

He visited Israel (then known as Palestine) in the 1930s and again in the 1950s for promoting the *Aliyah* of Cochin Jews and brought their case before the then Prime Minister of Israel. There is a photograph of my grandfather and Prime Minister Moshe Sharett of Israel[5] taken during a meeting in Jerusalem.

(This photograph was hanging until recently in the house of the late Gumliel and Reema Salem, in Mattancherry. The house was sold in 2019 to a boutique hotel group which refurbished it as a 10-room boutique guest house named Salem House.) - Bala Menon

---

5 Moshe Sharett was the second prime minister of Israel - 1954 to 55 - and served later as foreign minister under David Ben-Gurion. He was also the foreign minister during the 1948 Arab-Israeli war.

CHAPTER III

The Story Of Avo

Jew Town woke up one morning sometime in the mid-1750s or so to learn that a woman was sitting on the steps at the synagogue door with a child rolled up in a tattered blanket. Her clothes and thin frame indicated she had travelled a long distance and had not eaten proper food for a long time. Her long brown hair framed an attractive face.

The warden of the synagogue and community chief Yosef Hallegua Mudaliar was summoned and the elders met to discuss the matter. (*Mudaliar* or headman in Tamil was the title held by a senior/wealthy member of the Jewish community.[1])

They did not want to hand the woman and child over to the Raja's police force and she uttered only a few words in Hebrew, the words and accent different from what they knew from their synagogue rituals. She said her name was Kadhoori and that she was looking for work. She did not want to talk.

---

1 (The title of *mudaliar* or headman of the Jewish community, was first granted to the most prominent member of the Paradesi community by the Raja of Cochin in the mid-sixteenth century. The *Mudaliar* could settle minor disputes within the community and represent them in the court. By the end of the 17th century, the title had passed on to the Hallegua family. The title vanished after the Cochin Kingdom acceded to the Indian Union, although Samuel Hallegua (born 1931) remained the unofficial head of the community until his death in September 2009).

The Kadhoorie name belongs to an illustrious Mizrahi Jewish family from Baghdad. They were well-established in Bombay in the 18th century and later moved to Hong Kong and Shanghai. There is speculation among the Cochin Jews that Kadhoori was an indigent Baghdadi Jewish woman who landed in Jew Town with her daughter for unknown reasons. (A school named Sir Elly Kadhoorie School still runs in Mazagon, Mumbai, under Bene Israeli management.)

American writer Ida Cowen also mentioned a Kadhoorie link with Cochin in her book *"Jews in Remote Corners of the World"*. She was in Cochin in 1961 and wrote: "Accompanying me on that first visit to the Paradesi Synagogue was the community's leader, Dr. Shabbetai Samuel Koder, of the Indian branch of the well-known Kadoorie family."[2] No other details are given.

It was a time of great prosperity for the Paradesi Jews. Cochin was under the commercial and political influence of the Dutch East India Company (*Vereenigde Oost-Indische Compagnie* or VOC, as it was called) and had appointed Jew Town's Ezekiel Rahaby as its chief agent. The Jews were also close to the Cochin Royal Family and were consulted on many issues related to government and internal palace matters.

One of the wealthy Paradesi families offered to take Kadhoori in as a slave or servant and the matter was closed. Nobody came looking for Kadhoori and she didn't venture out of Jew Town ever.

It is said that, as the years went by, the daughter (whose name remains a mystery) metamorphosed into a beautiful young woman and caught the fancy of either the master of the household or one of his sons. Jew Town lore says the man's name was David and he was a respected figure in the community and known by the name of 'Daikachan'.

David did not marry her because of her low social standing as the daughter of a servant but he loved her deeply and remained faithful to her throughout his life. She bore him four sons and a daughter Hannah, who grew up to be as beautiful as her mother.

After the death of David (Daikachan), the sons tried to protect

2 Cowen, Ida. *Jews in Remote Corners of the World*, Prentice-Hall, Englewood Cliffs, New Jersey, 1971, pg 194.

their sister from the predatory hands of some Paradesi Jews, but they could not hold out for long.

Ruby Daniel wrote in her book that a cousin of Daikachan, the then community chieftain Shelomi Hallegua (Shlomo or Solomon) Mudaliar, became obsessed with Hannah and even gave up food and drink; he confined himself to his bedroom because her brothers would not agree to give her hand to him.

Shelomi could not legally marry Hannah as she was not considered truly Jewish - and some Paradesis of the day said she belonged to a foreign family of manumitted slaves or *meshuchrarim*.

A. B. Salem's third son Gumliel said the family of his great-great-grandfather Shelomi Hallegua then hatched a conspiracy to trap Hannah. Some of the younger Paradesi girls organized a party at one of their homes, which she was persuaded to attend. The trusting Hannah was then pushed into a room upstairs and Shelomi was sent in to speak with her. He entered the room and locked it from within.

Social mores of the day frowned on the mingling of single men and women and being alone with a man in a closed room was a disgrace for Hannah's brothers who, it is said, all left Jew Town, most probably to Bombay. "Nothing was heard about them again," said Gumliel. "Many of our community at that time went to Calcutta to work in Baghdadi Jewish companies and also to Rangoon as workers and small traders. They must have also migrated to those places. We have had several visitors to Jew Town, saying their grandfathers were from Cochin, but had no details of their lineage and most had no knowledge of Malayalam."

Shelomi was not allowed to marry in the Paradesi Synagogue, so he took Hannah to his private plantation island of Vettakka, where he recited words equivalent to a marriage vow *"Are at me-kudeshet li"* (Behold, you are holy to me).

Hannah and Shelomi lived together for 40 happy years and raised five children - a son and four daughters - named Avraham, Rachel, Sarah, Leah and Rivka. As Hannah grew older, she was addressed by everyone in the community as Annochimuthi (*muthi* is grandmother in Malayalam).

The union was not recognized by the Paradesis although Hannah had been granted a bill of manumission in 1826. The legal Jewish document stipulated that her sons would be counted in the *minyan*, the 10-men quorum required for synagogue prayers.[3]

These five children and their descendants were derided in the community as *meshuchrarim* (manumitted slaves) or the so-called Brown Jews, while remaining a part of the Paradesi Jewish congregation.

"The son Avraham grew up to become famous as the firebrand Avo or Avomutha in 19th century Cochin Jewish history. Avo was the grandfather of Abraham Barak Salem and my great grandfather," Gumliel said.

However, for reasons unknown, Shelomi took another wife, this time from the Paradesi community. Some say it was pressure from his relatives who did not accept Hannah as his wife; other stories say Hannah had started losing her mental faculties, isolated from society and living a lonely life on the Vettakka plantation. She asked Shelomi to get married again.

Shelomi's second wife gave birth to a son named Isaac Hallegua. Hannah was forced out of her marriage and her house on the Vettakka estate and she moved, along with her children into two houses on Synagogue Lane in the middle of Jew Town. (These houses were midway between the Paradesi Synagogue and the now-abandoned Kadavumbhagam Synagogue in the south end of Jew Street).

Avraham looked after the estates and the vast wealth of Shelomi Mudaliar, multiplying them through wise investments, acquisitions and efficient management. When Shelomi was on his deathbed after some years, Avraham was summoned and a promise extracted that he would take care of his step-brother Isaac.

One of the illustrious Jewish families at that time in Jew Town was the Doikas, who had come from Cranganore in the early 16th century, and who could trace their ancestry to the days of the legendary Chera Emperor Bhaskara Ravi Varman and the Jewish merchant Joseph Rabban.[4]

The Doikas were wealthy and they arranged to get their daugh-

---

3 Rabinowitz, Louis. *Far East mission,* Johannesburg: Eagle Press, 1952, pg 112.

4 Circa 1100 AD, according to tradition and historical records.

ter married to Avraham. The oral history of their descendants suggests that Avraham and the Doika family had a close relationship, and Avraham and his wife had five children who were at that time fully integrated into community life in Jew Town.[5]

Trouble began soon after, in the early 1840s, when some of the Paradesi Jews began introducing aggressive concepts of racial superiority, upsetting the social equilibrium of the tiny community in Cochin.

"Our family always got a raw deal in the community, then and in this century," said a bitter Gumliel. Avraham or Avo as he was known in Jew Town, was compelled to give away all shares in the family wealth to his step-brother.

There is scanty information about Avo or Ava as he has been sometimes called. Most European travellers who mentioned Avo had availed of the hospitality of the wealthier Paradesi Jews during their stay in Cochin and obviously chose only one side of the story. Two of the Hebrew books that mentioned Avo are by Jacob Saphir, who wrote *Eben Saphir* (vol. i., Lyck, 1866; vol. ii., Mainz, 1874) and Solomon Reinman who published his *Masaot Shelomo* (Vienna: W. Schur, 1884).

Jacob Saphir (1822–1886) was a rabbi and traveller of Romanian or Lithuanian descent (birthplace: Oshmiany) whose family moved to Safed. Saphir later settled in Jerusalem where he was asked by the city's Jews in 1848 to travel abroad to collect alms for the poor and funds for building the Hurva Synagogue in the Jewish Quarter. It was on a second trip in 1854 to the East that he landed in Cochin.

In his *Eben Saphir* (Sapphire Stone), Saphir wrote glowingly about Cochin's Jew Town, its inhabitants and the Paradesi Synagogue. However, he termed the Jews of the Thekkumbhagam and Kadavumbhagam synagogues on the same street as descendants of converted slaves.

Saphir also wrote about the divisions within the Jews of Cochin. In Volume 11, Chapter 23, he described the social hierarchy of the time. Saphir talked about Avo as the eldest son of wealthy Paradesi landlord Shlomo Hallegua through a manumitted slave. However, things came to a head when Shlomo's other son born to a 'pure'

5 Daniel & Johnson, *Ruby Of Cochin*, pg. 12.

Paradesi woman claimed the entire inheritance, including the fabled estate at Vettakka.

Saphir wrote: "[Avo asked his step-brother, the younger Hallegua] ...Am I not your elder brother, for thus my mother told me that your father was my father...And why cannot I also inherit the possessions of the house of our father?"[6]

Avo's opponents in the community, however, stood firm on their demand that he surrender his entire inheritance.

The dispute was taken to the Maharaja of Cochin, who decided in favour of Isaac Hallegua. Avo was evicted from the Vettakka estate and forced to look for employment.

Another story, as told by Ruby Daniel and Gumliel Salem says that Avo willingly gave away all the property, thinking that he could manage with what he had.

He was mistaken, however, and he did not think about his sisters or their children and their share in Shelomi Mudaliar's wealth. Ruby Daniel recounted: "...he did not realize that his own sisters, who became widows early, with their children would need help."[7]

The sisters did not have happy lives. One of them named Leah was only 16 when her husband died in a shipping accident off the Chinese coast near Shanghai, possibly working for the Baghdadi Jews of Calcutta.

Another sister Rivka also lost her husband in a shipping accident and was left to look after a daughter whom she brought up alone. This daughter died giving birth to a son who was then brought up by Rivka. The boy, Koko, left Jew Town when he became an adult and did not keep contact with Jew Town. He was believed to have lived and died in Bombay or Calcutta or Rangoon.

There was another sister Sarah, according to Ruby Daniel, who married a Jew called Binyamin Benaya, who came to Cochin from Yemen. Here the relationships get a little complicated. "[Sarah and Binyamin got a son named Benaya Benjamin and a daughter named Rivka. Rivka was the mother of both my grandmother

---

6 Saphir, *"Ha Yehudm b'Kogin'*, p30. Cited by Katz Nathan & Goldberg Ellen, *The Last Jews of Cochin: Jewish Identity in Hindu India,* University of South Carolina Press, 1993. pg 149.

7 Daniel & Johnson, *Ruby of Cochin*, pg 13.

Docho and my father Eliyahu Hai Daniel and I am named Rivka after her. The other sister, Rachel married a man named Haim and their son was my grandfather Daniel." [8]

The split in the Cochin Jewish community was wide open at this time and Avo and others like him were addressed as 'descendants of slaves'. Although *meshuchrarim* means freed or manumitted slaves, an influential section of Paradesis refused to recognize them as true Jews, portraying them as converts or illegitimate progeny of the 'white' Jews born through female servants or *yeled bayit* (child born in the house).

This genesis of oppression began two centuries earlier, with the arrival of European Jews in Cochin, fleeing the Inquisition in Spain and Portugal, sparked by the Alhambra Decree of 1492.[9]

They became known as the Paradesi Jews or Foreign Jews. They were welcomed in Jew Town by the Jews who were already settled there and most became part of the Thekhumbhagam congregation, which had a synagogue in the middle of Jew Street. It is believed that this synagogue was attended by the *meyuchasim* (Jews of noble lineage), who had arrived in Cochin after the destruction of their original Jewish home in Cranganore.

There was another synagogue at the far north end of the street called Kadavumbhagam which belonged to a congregation of Jews who apparently had no aristocratic background.

Soon, the Portuguese tactic of dividing the inhabitants of Cochin into black, brown and white began having its effect in Jew Town as well. The harsh caste system of Kerala at the time also added to the matrix, creating the first wedge within the community. The 'White Jews' or 'Paradesis' split from the Thekhumbhagam congregation and persuaded the Raja of Cochin to give them permission to build their own synagogue in 1568 - the Paradesi Synagogue, adjacent to the Raja's personal Krishna temple.

The converted servants and slaves of White Jews and their offspring became the first of Cochin's *meshuchrarim* or the manumit-

---

[8] Ibid, pg 13.

9 Isabella I of Castile and Ferdinand II of Aragon issued the Alhambra Decree of the Edict of Expulsion on March 31, 1492, expelling all practising Jews from their territories. The edict was revoked only in 1968.

ted ones, with few social and religious rights.

From the mid-16th century to the late 19th century Jewish scholars from Cairo and Jerusalem - through their many responses - questioned this behaviour and urged the Paradesi community to allow full privileges to the *meshuchrarim*, but the rulings were all ignored. Several of the *meshuchrarim* reportedly joined the Thekhumbhagam Synagogue, just metres away from the Paradesi Synagogue. (*It is pertinent to note here that the Paradesi meshuchrarim themselves did not socially or by marriage mingle with the so-called Black Jews or Malabari Jews, whom they considered inferior in social and religious status!*)

American Jewish scholar Dr. Nathan Katz and his wife Ellen Goldberg - who were instrumental is conducting the most definitive research on the Cochin Jews - have written about his host in Jew Town, A. B. Salem's second son Raymond Salem, and quoted him as saying (in 1987): "...I'd always assumed Jews were instrumental in designing the apartheid system, not in striving against it. Why, here in Jew Town, they devised their own system of apartheid against their fellow Jews."[10]

Talking about A. B. Salem, "Raymond dramatically concluded, [that] his father ultimately could not reverse what was to be Cochin's destiny: 'These people are cursed for their actions. It is this curse that explains the death of the Jew Town community." [11]

They were told that they could not have equal rights in the synagogue, although they were regular members of the congregation. In violation of *halakha* or Jewish law, they were asked to sit on the floor during prayers and not allowed to ascend the pulpit or recite certain prayers.

An entry made in the Paradesi record books in 1757 reads: "If an Israelite or Ger [convert] marries a woman from the daughters of the Black Jews [Malabaris] or the daughters of the *Meshuchrarim*, the sons who are born to them go after the mother; but the man, the Israelite or Ger, he stands in the congregation of our

10 Katz and Goldberg, *The Last Jews of Cochin*, pg 127.

11 Katz and Goldberg. Jewish "Apartheid" and a Jewish Gandhi, *Jewish Social Studies*, Vol. 50, No. 3/4 (Summer, 1988 - Autumn, 1993), pgs 147-176, URL: http://www.jstor.org/stable/4467422, pg 149.

community and he has no blemish...'[12]

Marriage with girls of the 'white' community was not allowed and after death, these 'Brown Jews' were not given permission to be buried in coffins and their graves had to be in the Black Jews' cemetery or after the advent of the 20th century in a distant, neglected corner of the Paradesi cemetery, alongside an outer wall. Scholars like J. B. Segal, Dr. Katz & Ellen Goldberg, David Mandelbaum, Walter Fischel and Dr. Barbara Johnson have written in detail about this social divide in the Paradesi community, so we won't delve too deep into the subject here.

Records dating to the 1760s show evidence of offspring of Paradesi men and slave women... 'A Paradesi census of early 1800s referred to such children as *yelide bayit* (children of the house) and they were considered distinct from slaves or manumitted slaves.'[13]

Katz also speculates that in time, the coloured Malabari Jews could have 'fallen out of favour with the Cochin Royal Family as well partly because they continued to be denounced [by the Paradesis] and gradually came to be viewed by other communities - as low caste slaves."[14]

Prof. P. M. Jussay, who was among the early researchers on the history of the Cochin Jews, wrote that after leaving their first settlement of Cranganore (Kodungalloor) and coming to Cochin : "...[they] gathered together as one united congregation first at Kochangadi Synagogue, built in 1345 and then at the Kadavumbhagam Synagogue built in 1550." However, age-old dissensions ... erupted again and Jews who came from Spain and handpicked Jews of 'pure lineage' built another synagogue in 1568. 'Thus the community split...'[15]

Dr. Katz and Goldberg have written in the *'Last Jews of Cochin'* that one of the visitors in 1828-1829 was Rabbi David D'Beth Hillel,

12 Katz and Goldberg. The Sephardi Diaspora in Cochin, *Jewish Political Studies Review* 5:3-4 *(Fall 1993).* pg 118.

13 Johnson, Barbara. *Our Community in Two Worlds, The Cochin Paradesi Jews in India and Israel*, Ph.D theses, University of Massachusetts, 1985, pg 73.

14 Katz and Goldberg. The Sephardi Diaspora in Cochin, *Jewish Political Studies Review* 5:3-4 (Fall 1993), pg 106.

15 Jussay, P. M. *The Jews of Kerala*, Calicut University, 2005.

who noted that Malabari Black Jews as having substantial wealth and an impressive religious life.

Several noted Rabbis from the middle of the 16th century onwards made pronouncements that *Halakah* or Jewish laws were being breached by the Paradesis in their treatment of the coloured Jews, even those who belonged to their synagogue... 'The Paradesi Jews contravened *Halakha* by creating a sub-caste and repeatedly defied rabbinic admonition and the censure of world Jewry.'[16]

Gumliel Salem said: "Under the leadership of my great grandfather Avo, the group rose up in revolt against this oppression in the synagogue and boycotted congregational meetings. They began praying in their houses, but this only angered the White Jews. They retaliated."

From the mid-16th century onwards, the leader of the Paradesi community, who held the title of *mudaliar* or chieftain conferred by an earlier Cochin ruler, controlled the day to day administration of the synagogue and affairs of the community. He could adjudicate on civil and criminal matters and the Raja could only intervene in case of capital offences or matters of state.

The White Jews complained to the Resident British governor that the sounds of the *shofar* (blowing of the ram's horn and the call to prayer) from private houses were disturbing regular proceedings in the synagogue.

The British Resident at the time was Lt. General William Cullen[17], who also held joint charge as Resident for the Kingdom of Travancore. Ruby wrote: "...one of the complaints was that there should not be a fourth synagogue in [Jew] town...The White Jews told him [the British Resident] that anyway these people don't need another synagogue, because they are welcome at our synagogue...

"The Resident, however, told the white Jews that he had measured the distance between the synagogue and the houses where

16 Katz and Goldberg, Jewish "Apartheid" and a Jewish Gandhi, *Jewish Social Studies*, Vol. 50, No. 3/4 (Summer, 1988 - Autumn, 1993), URL: http://www.jstor.org/stable/4467422, pg 148.

17 William Cullen was a British Army Officer with the Madras Artillery Regiment, and from 1840 to 1860 Resident in the Kingdom of Travancore and Cochin. He died at Allepey in Kerala, where a road is named after him.

private prayers were held and there was no possibility of any disturbance.[18] "

However, in 1842, the Diwan of Cochin Edakkunni Sankara Warrier[19] sided with the Paradesi synagogue and ordered that prayer services could not be organized by Avo and his 'group with impunity in the house appropriated for that purpose'. It was also ordered that the 'meshuchrarim should walk submissively to the white Jews.'[20]

In another blow, the Diwan rejected their plea for permission to build a separate synagogue in Jew Town on the ground that there were not sufficient members in the prayer group to set up a new place of worship.

Frequent verbal clashes began happening in Jew Town between the two groups, with Avo getting more aggressive with each passing day. Ruby Daniel wrote that after one such incident, the Paradesis hired some burly men from the nearby Kadavumbhagam congregation to beat up Avo's son Itzhak who was making a name for himself as a scholar and calligrapher. On a joyful Purim day, the thugs were plied with alcohol and sent to hunt for Itzhak and confiscate his treasured Sefer Torah.

They assaulted some women, but couldn't find Itzhak who hid in an attic. At a meeting that followed, Avo told his followers: "This is enough. Let us leave Jew Town". In 1848, the group moved en masse to Fort Cochin, about two kms away, which was under the control of the British resident, and settled in houses near the waterfront. Fort Cochin is one of the most scenic areas of Kerala, famous for its Chinese fishing nets and colonial-style homes, and streets lined with ancient trees.

In the early 18th century, however, during the Dutch sway in the kingdom, Fort Cochin was an exclusive enclave and people from Mattancherry were not allowed to settle in the area. The

18 Daniel & Johnson, *Ruby of Cochin*, pg 13.

19 Edakkunni Sankara Warrier, from a Nair family of Thrissur, served as the Diwan of Cochin from 1840 to 1856. He was considered a progressive and is credited with issuing a proclamation on February 16, 1856, abolishing slavery in the kingdom. His sons T. Sankunni Menon and T. Govindan Menon also served as Diwans of Cochin.

20 Johnson, Barbara, *Our Community in Two Worlds*, Ph.D theses, University of Massachusetts, 1985, pg 61.

policy had changed after the British wrested control from the Dutch and Avo and his followers were welcomed in Fort Cochin. "While the European population lived mostly within the fortified walls of Fort Cochin, Hindus, Muslims, Jews, Thomas Christians and Catholics lived around it... Even so, the walls were socially and economically permeable..."[21]

Members of Avo's group prospered in business, got themselves well-appointed homes and their women began flaunting gold jewellery and fashionable clothes. British missionaries offered educational facilities to the children and they also established their own synagogue in a building still called 'Synagogue House'.

"This structure is located in Lily Street, which today in known for its small, budget restaurants and home-stays for backpacking tourists. During the Dutch era, it was called Lelistraat, which became Lily Street after the British arrived and during the time of Avo," according to Mathew Antony, a grandson of A. B. Salem, who lives in the city of Ernakulam - across the bay from Mattancherry.[22]

Avo is also believed to have stayed in the backwaters town of Alleppey (today's Alappuzah) for some time - for business.

(Jacob Saphir wrote about visiting the Fort Cochin Jews in 1860 and performing a circumcision, which angered the White Jews of Mattancherry with whom he was staying.)[23]

It was a joyful world for Avo's group, far away from the oppression they faced in Mattancherry. Avo was the religious leader and ritual butcher (*sofer and shochet*) for the community. According to Ruby Daniel, her grandfather Eliyahu Japheth was about 12 years old when he was taken to Fort Cochin. She has written vividly about Jewish life in the settlement and how even young girls learned to read and write in convent-run schools - which was unheard of in the Mattancherry community.[24]

---

21 Singh, Anjana. *Fort Cochin in Kerala, 1750-1830: The Social Conditions of a Dutch Community*, Brill Academic Publishers, pg 42.

22 Antony, Mathew. Grandson of A. B. Salem, Rose House, Ernakulam. 2015, Personal communication.

23 Cited by Segal, J. B. *A History of the Jews of Cochin*, pgs 78-79.

24 Daniel & Johnson, *Ruby of Cochin*, pg 16.

However, tragedy struck Fort Cochin in the form of a virulent cholera epidemic, which killed most of the new settlers, about 75 of them, including Avo and his son Itzhak. They were all buried in a cemetery close to the beach, but the site has now disappeared. "We think the cemetery was close to the well-kept Dutch cemetery, near Lily Street and close to the beach. The site could have been encroached upon a long time ago," said Mathew.[25]

•••••

A few years ago, Mathew invited a noted Reiki practitioner and spiritual medium Poonam Bharti to make a tour of Fort Cochin and Mattancherry. In Fort Cochin, Mathew said, she stopped in front of several houses saying 'Jews lived here, Jews lived here and here and here and stopping in front of one of the houses she exclaimed: I can sense the spirit of Avo here."

(Poonam Bharti or Shaheen as she is also known, calls herself a 'Reiki grandmaster, spiritual counsellor and therapist.')

"I have completely surrendered myself in messages from Kryon, which is an empowering energy inviting human beings to participate physically, emotionally, and spiritually in the evolution of consciousness. It aims to help people orient and realign themselves to this energy.

"Kryon has nine channels around the world and I am the Kryon channel based at Mumbai since 1998."[26])

•••••

In Mattancherry, the Paradesis hailed the deaths of Avo and his group of Jews in Fort Cochin - saying it was divine punishment for abandoning their real family and congregation.

Solomon Reinman, who had become a member of the Paradesi congregation, wrote in his 'Masa'oth Shlomo b'Kogin': "G-d punished the sin of the meshuchrarim who were disloyal and withdrew from the synagogue of the White Jews and desecrated its holiness...almost all of the meshuchrarim died with the plague and epidemic.... and many became mad..."

"...The meshuchrar Avo who wrote the Sefer Torah died naked and for want of everything and his only son went out of his

25 Antony, Mathew. Personal communication, 2015.

26 Personal communication, February 2015.

mind..." And again: "...in this incident, we may see the divine approval of the White Jews' house of prayer, though justice was on the side of the *meshuchrarim*."[27]

Survivors of the epidemic found they could not conduct even basic synagogue services and soon dispersed. Many left to find jobs in Bombay and Calcutta while a few returned in shame to Mattancherry. (There are scores of Cochin Jewish graves in the Jewish cemetery in Calcutta - of Jews who left Cochin over many decades and their descendants.) The stragglers were readmitted into the Paradesi congregation after paying stiff fines and agreeing to be docile and submissive in their day-to-day religious and social lives. Most also continued to live in abject poverty.

Among them were Avo's mother Hannah, also known as Avochimutthi (who was once the 'Queen of Vettakka') and his daughters Belukka and Hannah.

Itzhak's son Japheth went to Calcutta and then sailed to England, where he failed in running a restaurant and catering business. He returned later as an old man to die in Mattancherry.

(Ruby Daniel says Japheth was buried in the Jewish Cemetery at Fort Cochin, after A. B. Salem made arrangements with the Cochin government to get it reopened for the purpose.).[28] But this could not be corroborated, because no one today knows the exact location of the cemetery.

Japheth's daughter Doris lived in Calcutta and disappeared from the radar of the Cochin Jews. Besides Itzhak, Avo had four other children - daughters Belukka and Hannah and sons Pichikaka and Thatcho (the last two were also believed to have died in the Fort Cochin epidemic because nobody seemed to have heard of them again). The many descendants of Hannah, who married a Yemeni scholar from Aden named Avraham, now live in various cities of Israel. Belukka, of course, lives on in history as the mother of her only son Abraham Barak Salem.

Japheth's sister Hannah married a Christian man named Pau-

---

27 'Solomon Reinman, *Masa'oth Shlomo b'Kogin*', cited by Katz & Goldberg, *The Last Jews of Cochin*, pg 150. Also cited in The Sephardi Diaspora in Cochin, *Jewish Political Studies Review* 5:3-4 (Fall 1993), pg 127.

28 Daniel & Johnson, *Ruby of Cochin*, pg 18.

lose in Cochin and they had a daughter called Ruth, who later re-converted to Judaism after marrying A. B. Salem, which created a controversy in Jew Town then and in later years.

The oppression and segregation of the *meshuchrarim* continued in Mattancherry, although slavery had been abolished by the British in 1833 and education was bringing about some enlightenment throughout the land. In the neighbouring kingdom of Travancore Queen Rani Lakshmi Bai (1811–1815) abolished slavery by a proclamation in 1813. Some years later, in 1854, Raja Ravi Varma IV (1853–1864) did the same in the Cochin Kingdom.

In 1882, one of the senior survivors of the Fort Cochin epidemic, Elias Avraham, petitioned the Diwan[29] again, seeking permission to build their own synagogue. He presented a supporting letter from one of the most prominent Jews of India at the time, industrialist David Sassoon from the Baghdadi congregation of Bombay. The petition was rejected, citing the precedent set in 1848.[30]

An 1895 report in an American newspaper said: "The Cochin Jews [still] make this distinction between those Jews born purely of Jewish parents and those born of alien mothers; those born of purely Jewish mothers being called "White" Jews and "White" Israelis, while those born of alien mothers are called "Black" Jews... the term Black is designated to denote a mixture of blood and... not the complexion..."[31]

A British missionary who visited Cochin in the mid-19th century wrote: "...even to this present time, Hindoos of Cochin become converts to Judaism. They consider themselves as slaves to the white Jews; paying them a yearly tribute, and they are bound to pay them a small sum for the privilege of having their children circumcised, and for being allowed in prayer-time to wear the phylacteries, called *Tefillin*. They do not sit down in the presence of the white Jews, nor eat with them..."[32]

29 Thottakattu Govinda Menon, Diwan of Cochin Kingdom from 1879 to 1890.

30 Johnson, Barbara, *Our Community in Two Worlds*, pg 63.

31 *The American Israelite*, Cincinnati, September 12, 1895, page 4; Quoted from the *Times of India*, Bombay (issue date not specified)

32 Wolff, Joseph Rev. *Travels and Adventures*, Saunders, Otley and Co., London, 1861, pg 462.

It must be mentioned here that the Paradesis also had running feuds with the Malabari Jewish congregations across the bay in Ernakulam and neighbouring areas over assertions of religious and racial purity. Latter-day scholars said that they partly appropriated the history of the Malabari Jews and made it their own, even tracing their ancestry to the original Jewish settlement in Cranganore (modern-day Kodungalloor).

The impeccable language skills of the Paradesis and contacts with European Jews ensured that it was their versions of Cochin Jewish history that was heard across the Jewish world. One of the stories that made the rounds in the 19th century was highlighted in the 'Israelite,[33] which reported "...that about 10,000 Jews were carried away [from Jerusalem]...accompanied by a host of black slaves, who killed their masters on their way and took possession of their property, but remained faithful to Judaism, which they adopted shortly before their treachery and massacres were resolved upon..." These slaves apparently became the first settlers, now known as the Malabari Jews.

In 1907, The Jewish Yearbook reported that "...the Black Jews of Cochin ... are divided into two classes: — Shechorim (blacks) and Meshuchrarim (emancipated slaves). The Meshuchrarim are not permitted to practise Jewish rites till they have obtained a certificate of manumission from their masters."

The report goes on to say that the question of the racial purity of the meshuchrarim was referred to Rabbi Phanizal, Chief Rabbi of Jerusalem, who ruled that the Shechorim ranked with ordinary Jews, but the Meshuchrarim must first undergo the ritual bath, a decision which was not accepted.

The report, however, says: "Although the relations between the blacks and the whites were formerly very embittered, they have grown more harmonious in modern times, and a Hebrew school is now attended by the children of both communities."[34]

•••••

The Malabari Jews were also not saintly in their dealings with

---

33 The Israelite - August 22, 1862 Black Jews, citing Mikwa Israel, pg 35.

34 The Jewish Yearbook, 'Colonial Synagogues And Institutions'. Edited Bt Rev. Isidore Harris, M.A. London, 1907, pg 233.

their own manumitted slaves, who were kept at arms' length in their many synagogues and in social life.

They were called *orumakkar* ('those alongside' in Malayalam) and did not enjoy ritual equality and were subordinate to the superior Malabari Meyuchasim. Dr. Barbara Johnson says that a prominent member of the Malabari community told her that they did have slaves and gave the example of one Pallathungal family from the Thekkumbhagam congregation in Ernakulam who had converted a large number of their slaves to Judaism.[35]

Prof. P. M. Jussay wrote that in the wealthy Malabari Jewish congregation of Paravur: "...casteism was virulent. The congregation had a few Jews who were considered lowborn. Others treated them unjustly. But the lowborn were wealthy and well-educated. So they demanded equal rights in all matters, including the administration of the synagogue... Every attempt to bring about a compromise failed and the matter was taken to a court of law. This went on until the chief protagonists left for Israel in the 1950s".[36]

Jussay also talked about another congregation at Mala, that "consisted of pure unadulterated black Jews... and the *meshuchrarim* or lowborn were treated unjustly by denying them equality with others even in the synagogue. So they formed themselves into a new congregation... they soon became a well-knit unit and had their own synagogue. They ran a leather curing centre..."[37]

•••••

In Bombay, the Baghdadi Jews who came to India in the 18th century treated the ancient Bene Israelis with contempt, denied them beds in a hospital built with their donations and burial in their cemetery.

(In an interesting development, the genetic history of the Cochin Jews were presented in a research paper in the journal 'Human Genetics' in 2016. The researchers used 'comprehensive genome-wide analyses, based on several high-end tests'. They found 'considerable Jewish genetic ancestry... [and] a significant recent

35 Johnson, Dr. Barbara. *Shingly or Jewish Cranganore in the Traditions of the Cochin Jews of India*, MA Theses, May 1975.

36 Jussay, P.M. Prof. *The Jews of Kerala*, pg 37.

37 Ibid, pg 43.

Jewish gene flow into this community 13-22 generations ago... with contributions from Yemenite, Sephardi and Middle Eastern Jews..."[38])

(DNA tests conducted on the Bene Israelis have also confirmed that they possessed 'in high frequency, the so-called Cohen Gene - CMH - s specific Y-chromosome haplotype that, with other indicators, evidences ancient Semitic/Hebrew ancestry.[39])

•••••

This type of overt discrimination was practised in all the Jewish congregations of Cochin despite several rulings by scholars. As early as the 1520s, Rabbi David ben Solomon ibn Abi Zimra of Cairo[40] declared that intermarriage was allowed between all Jews provided the so-called lowborn submitted to an immersion ritual.

Rabbi Jacob de Castro of Alexandria[41] also decreed several decades later that discriminatory behaviour by Jews in Cochin violated Jewish laws. These rulings were all ignored by the 'highborn' Jews.[42]

---

38 Waldman YY, Biddanda A, Dubrovsky M, Campbell CL, Oddoux C, Friedman E, Atzmon G, Halperin E, Ostrer H, Keinan A. The genetic history of Cochin Jews from India, *Human Genetics*, July 2016. Article published with open access at Springerlink.com - https://www.ncbi.nlm.nih.gov/pmc/articles/PMC5020127/pdf/439_2016_Article_1698.pdf

39 Report in *Times of India*, July 20, 2002. No sources cited in report.

40 David ben Solomon ibn Abi Zimra (1479–1573), also known as Radbaz, was Chief Rabbi of Egypt for 40 years. He was the author of over 3,000 responsa (interpretation of *halakhic* or Jewish law).

41 Rabbi Jacob de Castro (1525–1610), a disciple of Radbaz, was the last Chief Rabbi of Egypt to have wide influence among the Jews.

42 Cited by Segal, J. B in *A History of the Jews of Cochin*, pgs 24-25. From Marx, A. *A Contribution a l'histoire des Juifs de Cochin*, 1930-31.

CHAPTER IV

Salem - The Early Years

After the cholera epidemic in the second half of the 19th century, Avo's daughters Belukka and Hannah lived in a small house on the street just outside of Synagogue Lane, along with their mother, away from the White Jewish homes.

The family history goes a little murky at this juncture - and there are few records available to the public.

Hannah married a Jew from Aden, while Belukka became the wife of a Jew from Turkey. Several sleazy stories were spread about Belukka by Avo's antagonists at the time, all of which have been debunked by the Salem family. These were reported by South African Rabbi Louis Rabinowitz.[1]

A son born to Belukka and Barak on April 24, 1882, was named Avraham Baruch Salem,[2] and he became a towering personality among the Cochin Jews in the 20th century, his fame crossing the boundaries of the Cochin Kingdom and sparkling, albeit briefly, in the upper reaches of volatile Indian national politics. In Cochin, he also came to be known as the 'Jewish Gandhi' for his passionate es-

---

1 Rabbi Louis Rabinowitz in his book *Far East Mission*, pg 119. The rabbi pointed out that aspersions on Salem's legitimacy were cast when his second son Balfour was getting married to a girl from a wealthy Paradesi family.

2 Avraham for grandfather Avo, Baruch means 'blessed' in Hebrew and Salem from the Hebrew 'Shalom' meaning peace.

pousal of Gandhian methods of non-cooperation and non-violence as the moral way to fight injustice.

Salem was born in the same year that the Chief Rabbi of Palestine Raphael Meir Panigel sent an emissary Asher Levy[3] to Cochin to look into the discriminatory practices in Mattancherry.

(Levy came at the request of the Baghdadi Jews of Bombay who were allegedly being pressured by the Paradesis to withdraw privileges to a Cochin Jew, Benyamin Benaya, who was the son of Avo's friend Benyamin from Fort Cochin. Ruby Daniel wrote about the insulting behaviour and attempted assault on Levy by the Paradesis when he asked that the *meshuchrarim* be accepted as equals.[4])

Belukka brought up the child alone and was determined to give him an education. It is said that she had no money to buy enough kerosene to fire up the small lamps in her home - and little Salem had to sit outside and read books under the gloomy diffusion of street lamps on Jew Street. The lamps were stone receptacles for oil, bolted to the walls of homes and lit at night.

The closely-packed row houses were mostly inhabited by members of the Kadavumbhagam congregation on the far north end of the street. The small houses had verandahs or covered porches from where the Jews sold poultry, eggs, vinegar and groceries. Between some of the Jewish homes were Hindu and Muslim homes as well, most of them petty traders and artisans.[5]

•••••

From the south end, Salem's wealthy relatives among the Paradesi Jews ignored the destitute family and did not extend any financial assistance, 'although they received a small allowance from money kept aside for the needy from the synagogue'.[6]

It was at this time that the enlightened ruler of Cochin, Raja Rama Varma (1864-1888), and his Diwan Sankunni Menon estab-

----

3 Asher Abraham ha-Levi was born in Galicia in Spain. He travelled through the Balkan countries and then to India, where he settled in a town in the Himalayas. An account of his travels. *Harpatka'otav shel Asher ha-Levi*, was published in 1938.

4 Daniel & Johnson, Ruby of Cochin, pg 19.

5 Mandelbaum, David, The Jewish Way of Life in Cochin, *Jewish Social Studies, Vol. 1, No. 4* (Oct., 1939), Indiana University Press: http://www.jstor.org/stable/4464305 pg 440.

6 Gumliel Salem, personal communication, Mattancherry, March 2012.

lished English schools in each district of the Kingdom and set up reading rooms in Ernakulam - across the bay from Mattancherry. In Cochin, the first English school was started for British residents by Rev. J. Dawson, who opened an English-medium school - at Mattancherry in 1818. The school received a grant-in-aid from the Maharaja but closed after three years because it could not attract students. The Cochin government then started another school for teaching English, Hebrew and Malayalam to the children of the Jews the same year.

The Raja had passed orders that graduates in law and barristers needed to be appointed to higher positions in the government and that English common law become the framework for the government. The policies were continued by the next ruler Raja Veera Kerala Varma (1888-1895) and by Raja Rama Varma Thampuran, who ruled Cochin from 1895 to 1914.

The stage was set for young Salem for a career in law and politics.

•••••

Salem began schooling at the Protestant Mission School in Mattancherry and later at the Santa Cruz Secondary School. Being a devout Jew, he sent a request to the Education Director to be exempted from writing an exam on Sabbath, a petition that was accepted, while he was studying for his Intermediate undergraduate degree at Maharaja's College in Ernakulam.[7] He got scholarships all through his school and college years because of his high grades.

He completed his studies in 1901 and was keen on going to Madras for higher education but did not have the monetary wherewithal to do so.

Salem describes in his own words[8] (after he became a founding-member of the Cochin Legislative Assembly) the debt he owed to the 'great soul P. Rajagopalachari', then Diwan (Prime Minister) of the Cochin Kingdom.

"I approached [Diwan Rajagopalachari] as a forlorn boy just

7 Cited by Prof. Chiryankandath, James. "Nationalism, religion and community: A. B. Salem, the politics of identity and the disappearance of Cochin Jewry", *Journal of Global History* (2008), pg 27.

8 Proceedings of Cochin Legislative Council, December 12, 1927, *Kerala Archives*.

come out of the Ernakulam College and stopped at [his house] Krishna Vilas... as a Jewish student.

"I told him, 'Sir, I stand in need of education, I have no money to study,' and the great soul, in three hours' time, ...he issued a memorandum... of giving me the grant of a liberal scholarship to pursue my studies at Presidency College in Madras."

•••••

Long-distance travel was arduous in the early part of the 20th century. Salem had to travel about 100 km from Ernakulam/Cochin to Shoranur by bullock cart and boat and then take the Pattambi-Podanur steam railway (which was operational since 1860s - Podanur is near the Tamil Nadu city of Coimbatore). He then had to board another train from Podanur to Madras.

(The growth of railways in the Cochin Kingdom only began with the extension of the Shoranur line to Ernakulam in 1902 after a trilateral agreement was signed between the Kingdom of Travancore, Cochin and the British Resident. The Cochin State railway, 64.75 miles long, was opened as meter gauge in July 1902. The Shoranur-Ernakulam line was opened the same year.)

Soon after his arrival in Madras and while pursuing his studies, he took up a job as an 'Appeals Examiner' in the Madras High Court at a salary of Rs. 50 a month, a handsome sum in those days.

However, the restless Salem applied for government training and was offered a job in the Fisheries Department of the Madras Presidency. He saw this as an entirely new field and spent two years as Special Staff Member of an investigation team looking into the condition and potential for fisheries in the Presidency, along with continuing with classes for his law degree.

Salem returned to Cochin after his studies in 1905, completing his Bachelor of Arts and later getting a Law degree from Presidency College - thus becoming the first Jewish advocate in the Cochin Kingdom.

He was appointed Officer on Special Duty for Fisheries of the Cochin Kingdom - from 1907 to 1909 - based on reports about his exemplary work while in Madras.

He wrote two definitive papers as part of special assignments, which were published by the government in 1909, a 19-page document on *"The Fishing Stakes of Cochin"* and a nine-page brief on *"Inland Fisheries of Cochin."*[9]

American journalist Ida Cohen, who met him in Cochin, said: "Then he gave up this job, saying characteristically: 'Government service is not for me; it's only for psychopaths...' [10]

His rebellious streak was already emerging as he began pondering over social and economic ills and divisions within society. He opened his own law practice and began to attract clientele from every stratum of society - both Jews and non-Jews.

He shone in different cases at the local District and Sessions Court and at the Cochin Higher Court in Ernakulam. He was also being recognized as an articulate leader of the Jewish community and residents of Mattancherry town who began approaching him with petitions to intercede on their behalf with various levels of government and the sluggish bureaucracy.

This wider interaction allowed him to take his first steps into the world of politics. In 1910, Salem's name was announced in the Cochin Government Gazette as the first president of the Mattancherry Town Council, which had just been established.

His sojourn in Madras had broadened his world-view and he had come into contact with several men of towering intellect like C. Rajagopalachari and John Mathai, who were close to Mahatma Gandhi and Jawaharlal Nehru. Rajagoplachari was later to become the first Governor-General of India, after the country got its independence in 1947, and Mathai was India's first Education Minister.

•••••

The early part of the 20th century was the period of enlightenment in Cochin. There were more than twenty newspapers and about a dozen weeklies in the Cochin kingdom, highlighting the stirring of nationalism in various parts of India and the different agitations and streams of political thought. Although the administration brought in a Press Law in 1912 and another draconian one in 1936, political debates centered around news reports created a fertile ground for populist movements.

---

9 The authors could not get hold of copies of these reports in Kerala or elsewhere.

10 Cohen, Ida. Cochin Jews - Their Fight for Equality, *The Canadian Jewish Chronicle* - April 5, 1963 - Friday, Passover Edition, Nisan 11, pg 91.

One of the strongest reform upheavals to shake the caste-conscious Kerala society of the time was the Temple Entry Movement, which began in the town of Vaikom in the south-central district of Kottayam, part of the Kingdom of Travancore. The roads near the famous Lord Siva Temple in the town remained barred to lower castes although it had been thrown open to all people through a notification by an earlier Maharaja[11] in 1865.

1n 1924-25, organized protests began at the site with joint delegations of all castes trying to gain entry into the temple. Mass leaders like Periyar Ramaswamy Naicker and Mahatma Gandhi were present at Vaikom, along with Sree Narayana Guru, the foremost leader of the Reformist movement. A huge procession led by the upper caste Nair leader Mannath Padmanabhan also went to the Royal Palace in Trivandrum[12] in support of the Vaikom protestors.

Salem made several mentions of these protests when he was a member of the Cochin Council.

The Vaikom movement inspired Congress leader K. Kelappan to start the temple entry Satyagraha (civil disobedience) in Guruvayoor in 1931, in today's Thrissur district. (Guruvayoor is the main temple town of Kerala, with its ancient Lord Krishna temple.)

Supporters of this movement organized a Trichur Temple Entry Satyagraha Committee. The Trichur movement and the agitational success of the Vaikom activists provided the impetus to Salem to launch his own struggle in the Paradesi synagogue so that the so-called meshuchrarim could become full members of the congregation.

---

11 Ayilyam Thirunal Rama Varma III (1860-1880) was considered a benevolent and able ruler. Travancore was during his reign called 'The Model State Of India.'

12 Travancore was at the time ruled by Regent Maharani Sethu Lakshmi Bayi, who came to power after the death of her uncle Maharaja Moolam Thirunal in August 1924. She ruled until 1931.

CHAPTER V

Synagogue Travails

In 1930, a member of the Cochin legislature, Ikkanda Warrier (who later became the first and last Prime Minister of Free Cochin in 1948) moved a resolution in the council: *"This council recommends to the government to throw open all the roads, schools, wells and tanks and temples maintained or subsidized by them and accessible to the caste Hindus to the non-caste Hindus."*[1]

On November 12, 1936, which was also his birthday, the young Maharaja of Travancore, Sri Chitra Thirunal Balarama Varma, issued a proclamation from his palace in Tiruvananthapuram. The proclamation said, in its entirety:

"Profoundly convinced of the truth and validity of our religion, believing that it is based on divine guidance and on all-comprehending toleration, knowing that in its practice it has throughout the centuries, adapted itself to the needs of changing times, solicitous that none of our Hindu subjects should, by reason of birth or caste or community, be denied the consolation and the solace of the Hindu faith, we have decided and hereby declare, ordain and command that, subject to such rules and conditions as may be laid down and imposed by us for preserving their proper

1 Proceedings of Cochin Legislative Council, August 5, 1930, *Kerala Archives.*

atmosphere and maintaining their rituals and observances, there should henceforth be no restriction placed on any Hindu by birth or religion on entering or worshipping at temples controlled by us and our Government."

•••••

One of the scholars in Jew Town during Salem's younger years was Eliyahu Japheth who taught the Torah to many of the Paradesi Jews (but was still considered an outsider in the synagogue). Japheth was the grandfather of Ruby Daniel who, along with Dr. Barbara Johnson, wrote about life in the Mattancherry community in the classic *Ruby of Cochin*. He was a close friend of Salem and both had long hours of philosophical arguments about Jewish law and its interpretations.

About the segregation in the synagogue, Ruby wrote: "...both the Salem family and our family had to sit separately from the others... the men in the *azarah* (entrance room/antechamber) and the women in a separate building just in front of the synagogue... it was a shame for us."[2]

Japheth stopped going to the synagogue except on Yom Kippur holy days, opting to pray at home.

Ruby characterized Salem as a man with a 'thick skin like an elephant' and who would constantly quarrel in the synagogue with other congregation members about his seating and other rights.

Once the warden and others wanted Salem and Japheth to sign an affidavit declaring themselves as *meshuchrar* and then petition for whatever they needed. Although Salem was willing, says Ruby, her grandfather argued: "They want us to bring it in the record that we accept the status, to make this record ourselves"[3] and refused to sign it although Salem persuaded him to do so.

Katz and Goldberg observe: "Not only were Paradesi *meshuchrarim* denied ritual equality, they could not chant certain liturgical hymns, be called to the Torah to recite prayers or read a portion of the Scripture, bury their dead in coffins or, for that matter, in the Paradesi cemetery - but they were also proscribed

---

2 Daniel & Johnson, *Ruby of Cochin*, pg 21.

3 Ibid, pg 22.

from marrying any members of the 'white' faction."[4]

•••••

In 1963, four years before his death, Salem narrated his life story to American journalist Ida G. Cowen[5] who was then visiting Cochin. She later wrote an article for *The Canadian Jewish Chronicle* about Salem, focusing on his 'battles' in the Paradesi Synagogue.[6]

It appears that this was the only interview he gave to any Western journalist/author. Although many Jewish scholars visited Cochin, they either did not meet with him because of his supposed abrasive nature or were dissuaded from meeting him by the leading members of the Paradesi community (as his son Gumliel liked to remind everyone.)

Cowen wrote: "At a Friday night service at the Paradesi Synagogue my gaze was drawn to a small, frail, brown-skinned, white-bearded man on a bench nearby... I was told he was A. B. Salem."

Cowen then wondered 'if this frail-looking, 80-year-old man was the doughty warrior who led the fight years ago to break the age-old tradition which had permitted the *meshuchrarim*, the coloured Jews of Cochin, to pray together with the White Jews - but only if they sat on the floor?'

Cowen went on to describe how she spoke with Salem for a few minutes after the service and realized that "here was a man of rich personality, of keen intelligence – and still a fighter for what he considered just and right. I met and talked with him a number of times. We walked along Jew Town road...We talked until I had pieced together the story of this courageous son of Israel."[7]

In a book published in 1971, four years after Salem's death, Ida Cowen devoted several pages to the Cochin Jews in a chapter on India. She wrote: "I was ... astonished at the first service at the Pa-

---

4 Katz and Goldberg. Jewish "Apartheid" and a Jewish Gandhi pg 165, *Jewish Social Studies,* Vol. 50, No. 3/4 (Summer, 1988 - Autumn, 1993), URL: http://www.jstor.org/stable/4467422

5 Ida G Cowen (1898 - 1993). Ida G Cowen's last known residence was in New York County, New York.

6 'Cochin Jews - Their Fight for Equality', *The Canadian Jewish Chronicle* - April 5, 1963 Friday, Passover Edition, Nisan 11, pg 91.

7 Ibid, pg 91.

radesi Synagogue to see Avraham Baruch Salem, an Emancipated Jew, sitting on one of the pews. How had integration come to the Paradesi? Brown-skinned, frail, gentle-voiced A. B. - as he was affectionately known to all - told me the story of his one-man fight for integration as we talked and walked along Jew Town Road."[8]

This was November of 1961, almost 30 years after Salem broke down the wall that prevented his people from becoming full members of the congregation.

Cowen quoted Salem as saying that how, at the height of his agitation, he held a one-man peaceful demonstration by deciding to pray at home on the Kol Nidre Eve. As other Jews made their way to the synagogue, 'they heard Salem call out, "I am not going to the Paradesi to pray with slaves. We were slaves unto Pharaoh in Egypt. Here I am a free man. No more sitting on the floor while the White Jews sit in the pews.'[9]

In *The Jewish Chronicle* article in 1963, Cowen wrote: "The *Meshuchrarim* and other black Jews were poor, economically dependent upon the White Jews. They might accept this mark of inequality, of slavery in silence. But not A. B. He thought *"Avadim havinu b'Mitzraim; we were slaves in Egypt. Here I am a free man. No more slavery for me."*[10]

•••••

Salem was impressed with the success being achieved by Mahatma Gandhi in the 1930s during the Indian civil disobedience movement that ignited non-violent rebellion across the country. He decided this tactic should work in the synagogue as well.

Outside Synagogue Lane, Salem was a respected figure in all of Cochin, a well-to-do lawyer, a political and trade union leader, who owned two houses near the synagogue and whose wife was a successful medical practitioner.

Wherever Salem went, people would get up from their seats as a mark of respect to greet him with folded hands. "He was fa-

---

8 Cowen, Ida. *Jews in Remote Corners of the World*, Prentice-HalL, Englewood Cliffs, New Jersey, 1971. pg 208.

9 Ibid, pg 209.

10 Cowen, Ida. Cochin Jews - Their Fight for Equality, *The Canadian Jewish Chronicle* - April 5, 1963 Friday, Passover Edition, Nisan 11, pg 92.

mous and popular. Even those who opposed his ideas were fond of him."[11]

The situation was different in the synagogue, where humiliation was heaped upon him and some others like him. While there was no social ostracism, there was religious exclusion, which was very hurtful to him.

British adventurer Thomas Lovell, who came to Cochin in 1930, wrote: "But by far the most interesting community we find in Cochin is in Jew Town... But such is the effect of India on invading religions that even Jews are split up into three separate castes, known as the 'Whites', the 'Browns' and the 'Blacks'."[12] He does not mention A.B. Salem in his book.

Salem was a devout Jew, proud of his identity, and always wore the kippa or yarmulke - the Jewish skullcap. He was also reasonably fluent in Hebrew and was appointed to serve on the University of Madras Board of Hebrew and Syriac studies and could tutor children in Jew Town.[13] (Most were children of those who opposed him within the synagogue.)

Salem and his group were not allowed to sit on the benches inside the synagogue and had to sit on the floor in the antechamber. He refused to do so and took the help of two of his sons Raymond and Balfour in his campaign. "... [they] were not called to the Torah to recite blessings or to read a portion of Scripture (they were allowed to read publicly from the Torah after the third aliyah, or blessing, only on Simchat Torah, and could not be honoured by being called up by name), or be buried in the Paradesi cemetery."[14]

In Gumliel Salem's words: "Dad fought back. He was known for his truculence. He took my brothers to the synagogue and made them sit on the steps leading to the sacred Ark. My brothers thought it was great fun."

---

11 Daniel & Johnson, *Ruby of Cochin*, pg 21.

12 Thomas, Lowell. *India: Land of the Black Pagoda*, P.F. Collier & Son Corp., New York, 1930, pg 32.

13 Chiryankandath, James. *"Nationalism, religion and community*... pg 28.

14 Katz and Goldberg, Jewish "Apartheid" and a Jewish Gandhi pg 165, *Jewish Social Studies,* Vol. 50, No. 3/4 (Summer, 1988 - Autumn, 1993), URL: http://www.jstor.org/stable/4467422

"On many days they also sat on the window sills inside the synagogue, shaking their legs vigorously and refusing to get down although they were constantly harangued. Then Dad would also shout back at those who came to confront them."[15]

On some days, Salem made the children sit on the benches - (which they were prohibited from using) and when anybody asked them to move, Salem would say: "The children are under my orders. They remain on the bench."[16]

He made an entry in his diary: "The synagogue question is becoming serious as the children of mine are being opposed in taking their legitimate seats inside..."[17]

Heated discussions were held on the issue, without any resolution. In another of his notes, Salem said: "There was a communal meeting last night to solve the disabilities of the so-called manumitted Jews of Cochin..."[18]

On many occasions, Salem would give up the fight and refuse to go to the synagogue, only to rake up the issue again after a few days. His strong character, integrity and determination soon came to be looked upon with admiration by the youngsters in the congregation, who had grown up hearing about Salem's reputation outside the confines of Jew Town.

Salem sought the support of community elder Eliyahu Japheth, who refused to be drawn into the battle. So Salem decided to go it alone. In 1932, on Shemini Azareth - the eighth day of the Sukkot festival, he decided to mount a full challenge and occupy the reserved benches. The day was special for one of the synagogue administrators whose son was to celebrate his Bar Mitzvah - coming of age ritual.

The administrator "suggested a compromise - let A. B. and the children take seats on the steps leading to the upper gallery where the Torah reading takes place. Salem refused to budge saying he

---

15 Salem, Gumliel. Personal communication.

16 Cowen, Ida. Cochin Jews - Their Fight for Equality, *The Canadian Jewish Chronicle*, pg 92.

17 Cited by Johnson, Barbara, from *Salem Diaries 10-6-30* in *Our Community in Two Worlds*, Ph.D Thesis, University of Massachusetts, 1985, pg 85.

18 Ibid. *Salem Diaries* 9-25-30.

and his sons would have to get up and down at least 14 times as each reader goes up and returns to his place on the main floor."[19]

The argument escalated until some younger members of the congregation also joined Salem and told the elders to settle the matter immediately and threatened to boycott the Simchat Torah celebrations and the ritual of carrying the Sefer Torah around the synagogue and Salem won the fight that day.

Ruby Daniel wrote of the concessions: "Anyway, when the white Jews finally decided to give the synagogue rights to our families, the first aliyah to the Torah was given to their teacher, my grandfather Eliyahu Japheth."[20]

Although Salem and his group were given many synagogue rights on that day in 1932, some aspects of ostracism continued and this was reflected in his public appearances.

During the Second Session of the Jews Conference held at their office premises in Ernakulam and presided over by A. B. Salem on New Year's Day in 1934, he flayed "the false notions of racial superiority and inferiority between the so-called 'White' and 'Black' Jews'.

Salem argued: "[This was creating] the most depressing environment which was not conducive to the growth of society..." He called for "the need to strengthen and consolidate the various institutions of the community" and pleaded for constructive and united action on the part of the Jews and that "the Jews must go through a process of self-introspection."[21]

He also railed against the attitude of the Cochin government in not helping them [the Jews] in their 'onward march of progress'. Resolutions aimed at communal unity and due representation in Government offices were passed during the session, attended mainly by the Jews of Ernakulam and surrounding areas.

•••••

David G. Mandelbaum (1911-1987) was an American social and cultural anthropologist who visited Cochin in 1937 and docu-

19 Cowen, Ida. Cochin Jews - Their Fight for Equality, *The Canadian Jewish Chronicle*, pg 92.

20 Daniel & Johnson, *Ruby of Cochin*, pg 21.

21 *The Indian Express*, Tuesday, January 2, 1934.

mented Jewish life in many articles, photographs and a widely acclaimed short film. Mandelbaum served with the U.S. Army in India and Burma during World War II and later taught at the University of Minnesota and the University of California, Berkeley. He is the author of *"Society in India: Change and Continuity."*

However, Mandelbaum strangely mentioned the name 'Salem' only twice in his acclaimed 1939 paper on *The Jewish Way of Life in Cochin,* although Salem was well-known and regarded as a senior leader by almost all the seven Cochin Jewish congregations. He wrote in a footnote: "Mr. A. B. Salem, who has traced the genealogies of many of the families, kindly provided me with the Cohen data. Mr. Salem has written and privately published an excellent description of the Paradesi synagogue."[22]

The data referred to the story of two Jews from Baghdad who were induced to join the Paradesi congregation in a bid to get a member of the priestly class or *kohen* to conduct proper services.

A Jacob David Cohen who visited Cochin in 1820 stayed on, marrying a Paradesi girl named Rachel, although he had a wife and daughter in Baghdad. After some years, his son Daniel reached Cochin searching for his father, and he too settled down to marry an Esther Moses from the well-known Sarphati family. The Daniel lineage flourished in Cochin and continued to the middle of the 20th century.

Without mentioning Salem or other members of the so-called *meshuchrarim,* Mandelbaum diplomatically opted to say that there was in Cochin a "third endogamous caste...who have been called brown Jews. They are the descendants of slaves who had been set free and fully admitted to Judaism. Among them also were the illegitimate children of white Jews and their native mistresses."[23]

These children who grew up free, he wrote, did not mix with the Malabari Jews, but stayed on with the Paradesis, although they were not allowed into the synagogue proper.

Mandelbaum acknowledged in his paper that the wealthy Kod-

---

20 Mandelbaum, G. David. The Jewish Way of Life in Cochin, *Jewish Social Studies,* Vol 1. No. 4, October 1939, pp 423-460. Indiana University Press. jstor url: http://www.Jstor. Org/stable/4464305 . Accessed: 01/01/2014 18:10, pg 437.

23 Mandelbaum, G. David. *The Jewish Way of Life in Cochin,* pg 437.

er family extended hospitality to him and 'enhanced the pleasure' of his stay in Cochin (S. S. Koder was one of Salem's antagonists in synagogue affairs but they were partners in many commercial ventures). Mandelbaum also thanks Dr. A. I. Simon (another of Salem's 'foes'), who helped with information about the community.

Mandelbaum heaped praise on Salem, but avoids mentioning the rebellious 'Salem' by name or his grandfather Avo, when he wrote, "This member [grandson of one who rebelled in the middle of the last century] of the *m'shuhararim* is one of the most learned, both in Hebrew and in English, of all the Jews of Cochin."[24]

Mandelbaum went on to add that HE [Salem] tried various approaches to resolve the issue of discrimination. "*HE* emulated Gandhi... by imposing a fast on himself and remaining in the synagogue while he was starving."[25]

However, after this method failed, "*HE* tried the more modern technique of the sit-down strike by planting himself on the narrow stairway which leads up to the reading desk of the synagogue and refusing to budge until his demands were granted. That led to a tussle but not to the desired outcome."[26]

•••••

An American traveller Harry Simonhoff who visited Cochin in 1950 described the Mattancherry community: "Today the visitor finds the Jewish community of Cochin divided into three segments... The cleavage... continues to our own day. Whether due to Spanish arrogance, or the caste system... the evils of separatism have also poisoned Indian Jewish life. The 'Whites' look down upon the 'Blacks'... they imposed social ostracism and even refused to admit them into the synagogue ritua ... the condition, though greatly improved, continues to stratify the community."[27]

(*Harry Simonhoff (1890-1966) was born in Lithuania, the son of Rabbi Jacob J. and Jennie (Shapiro) Simonhoff. He practised law in Charleston,*

---

24 Ibid, pg 449.

25 Ibid, pg 449.

26 Ibid, pg 449.

27 Simonhoff, Harry. *Under Strange Skies*, Philosophical Library, New York, 1953, pg 190-191. http://www.archive.org/stream/understrangeskie012439mbp/understrangeskie012439mbp_djvu.tx

South Carolina, and served two terms as a representative in the State Leg-
islature. He travelled across the world in 1950, documenting Jewish life
and publishing the book 'Under Strange Skies' in 1953.)

Simonhoff neglected to mention the name of A. B. Salem, or his struggles in this regard. He only made a passing mention of a mysterious 'follower of Mahatma Gandhi who staged passive resistance and threatened a hunger strike in the synagogue until the rights of Jewish law were accorded the Meshuchrarim."[28]

He wrote: "These *Meshuchrarim* are supposedly the descendants of freed slaves. Their religious rights were restricted in the synagogues of the two other communal groups. Though included in the *minyan*, the quorum of ten worshippers empowered to conduct a service, they were until recently denied the privilege of being married in the synagogue, or even sitting on its benches. Their burial in the 'White' Jews cemetery was forbidden."[29]

Simonhoff also did not meet with Salem. It is pertinent to note here that Simonhoff talked in an earlier paragraph that he was hosted in Cochin by S. S. Koder, the leader of the Paradesi community at the time and who was in charge of synagogue affairs.

Simonhoff went on, however, to rightly argue that "...we must not regard the several thousand Jews of Cochin as inhuman or sluggish. Caught in the pattern of Indian life, they also became victims of the [Indian] caste system."[30]

In 1937, Salem and his group were allotted two benches at the back of synagogue where they could sit. They could read the Law on weekdays but were not allowed to do so on Shabbat.

"That night inequalities were wiped out. That night, all Jews of Cochin, no matter what the colour of their skin, were accepted as equals at the White Jews' synagogue. That night, Simchat Torah in the year 1932 was a real Simchat Torah.

"Since that night, A. B. Salem and all Jews can join the service in God's house as equals, can sit on the benches and have all other synagogue rights. And since that night, the man who rose not from the ranks, but from the depths, A. B Salem, whose name signifies

28 Ibid, pg 192.

29 Simonhoff, Harry, *Under Strange Skies*, pg 192.

30 Ibid, pg 192.

peace, has fought other battles for peace and right."[31]

Ida Cowen, however, missed out on some facts or A. B. Salem might not have told her the full story.

When she wrote that all rights were given to Salem's group, it was only two benches in the synagogue that were reserved for them in a corner of the synagogue.

In 1937, David Mandelbaum had observed that the *meshuchrarim* was given the right to read from the Law on week days, but not on the Shabbat (although this changed by 1947).

"These allowances still did not satisfy the grandson of the original rebel. He has completely withdrawn from the synagogue and conducts the services by himself in his home, meticulously reciting the prayers in their entirety..."

Mandelbaum explained: "The caste division is not a fossil relic of the past but is a dynamic and biting force in the lives of the members of the community."[32]

According to Gumliel Salem, there were only about 30 or so so-called *meshuchrarim* in Cochin at that time and he vividly remembered the stories told to him of those days by elders in the community. Salem and his group were also not allowed to marry or hold circumcisions and other celebrations in the synagogue.

Rabbi Louis Rabinowitz, Chief Rabbi of the Transvaal, South Africa, who visited Cochin in 1951, wrote in a chapter titled 'Apartheid in Cochin' that Salem had collected lots of material regarding the rights of his class, showing how they were subjected to injustice and discrimination. "It was his threat of a fast-unto-death inside the synagogue that brought the recalcitrant elders to their knees."[33]

(Rabinowitz was born in Edinburgh, Scotland, the descendant of a long lineage of Lithuanian Rabbis. He served as rabbi in several London synagogues and was appointed Senior Jewish chaplain of the British Army during World War II, serving in the Middle East and during the Norman-

---

31 Cowen, Ida. Cochin Jews - Their Fight for Equality, *The Canadian Jewish Chronicle* - April 5, 1963 Friday, Passover Edition, Nisan 11, pg 93.

32. Mandelbaum, G. David. The Jewish Way of Life in Cochin, *Jewish Social Studies*, pg 450.

33 Rabinowitz, Louis. *Far East Mission*, Eagle Press, Johannesburg, 1952, pg 117.

dy Invasion. He went to South Africa in 1945 and soon became famous for publicly stripping his war decorations in protest against polices in British Palestine Mandate, He was also a critic of the South African National Party's apartheid policies. In 1961, he emigrated to Israel and worked on the Encyclopaedia Judaica and got involved in Jerusalem city politics. He was a founder of the Movement for a Greater Land of Israel and opposed the Israeli withdrawal from the Sinai Peninsula after the Camp David Peace agreements with Egypt.) [34]

Salem recorded in his journal: "For the first time in the history of the Paradesi Synagogue I got the chance, by stressing on the Law of the religious services regarding the reading of Torah, the privilege of reading the Maphtir of this Shabbat and Rosh Hodesh. May G-d be praised... May the innovation become the order of the day!"[35]

Salem, however, kept up the fight. In 1940, the synagogue elders relented and said the *meshuchrarim* could bury their dead in the Paradesi cemetery, but in a separate section. They were also allowed to read some sections from the Torah on Shabbat.

Rabinowitz, however, clarified that the rights granted were not full rights. Salem and his group were allowed only the least honourable fifth Aliyah and their burial was also against the wall at the far end of the cemetery 'separated from the main portion by a stinking, stagnant pond.'[36]

Prof. Jussay (*The Jews of Kerala*) wrote briefly about Avo, but only made a passing mention of A. B. Salem, although he must have known about him in the 1960s when he was talking to Jewish leaders in both the Paradesi and Malabari communities.

Salem was a famous name in the region, but Jussay strangely devoted only a single paragraph to Salem, saying that he employed the Gandhian method of fasting for getting his rights in the synagogue and that he was supported by youngsters in the Paradesi congregation.

Renowned Jewish activist Gerhart Riegner who travelled to Co-

---

34 Information from Wikipedia.

35 Cited by Johnson, Barbara, *Our Community in Two Worlds*, pg 85.

36 Rabinowitz, *Far East Mission*, pg 118. (The pond is gone now and the cemetery has been landscaped.)

chin in 1956 also dismissed Salem in one sentence without mentioning his name in his book 'Never Despair'. He wrote: "I also met the man who led the revolution of the black Jews against the White Jews..."[37]

It remains an enigma why Salem was driven into the shadows of Cochin Jewish history by supposedly objective visiting scholars - although he was a towering figure in the political, social and economic life of his own Mattancherry constituency and the larger Cochin Kingdom. Salem championed several causes both in the Cochin assembly and outside it throughout his life, but there were few people to champion for him.

---

37 Riegner, Gerhart. *Never Despair: Sixty Years in the Service of the Jewish People and of Human Rights*, Ivan R. Dee, Chicago, 2006, pg 414.

CHAPTER VI

Salem In Politics

As a lawyer in Cochin, Salem soon came to be known as a champion of the underprivileged, the poor dock workers, rickshaw pullers and those working in tile and brick factories in Mattancherry and the surrounding areas.

He began taking an interest in politics and gravitated to the All People's Association (Mahajana Sabha), founded in 1916 as a discussion body to liaise with the Cochin administration. It was dominated by wealthy landowners and traders, but Salem soon got an insight into the workings of the upper echelons of society.

The political winds throughout India began changing in 1919 after Mahatma Gandhi returned to India in 1915 at the invitation of pro-independence leaders. Gandhi had made a name for himself fighting Apartheid in South Africa and immediately found in India a fertile ground to propagate his theory of non-violent civil disobedience and non-cooperation.

The Mahajana Sabha submitted a proposal in 1919 to the Cochin government - asking for the creation of a legislative body comprising elected and nominated members. The proposal was accepted by Maharaja Rama Varma XVI (1915-1932).

In a parallel direction, Salem became a fixture at the raucous meetings of the newly-founded Travancore Labour Association and the Quilon Labour Association in the neighbouring Kingdom of Travancore.

His radical speeches were a hit at these gatherings, many of which he presided over. His colleagues at the time included Sardar K. M Pannikkar[1], the revolutionary Sahodaran Aiyappan[2], T. K. Madhavan[3] and the leader and founder of the Dravida Kazhagam, Periyar E. V. Ramaswamy Naicker[4], who changed the face of politics in the neighbouring state of Tamil Nadu after Independence.

In 1925, Salem was elected to the first Cochin Legislative Council from the Special Jewish Constituency.

While busy espousing a nationalist agenda in the putative Cochin legislature as an independent representative of his community, he was appointed as one of the first three secretaries of the Indian States' Peoples Party - a wing specially created by the Indian National Congress to be active in India's princely states.

He also became the Whip of the political grouping in the Cochin Council which called itself the Progressive Party.

1 Sardar Kavalam Madhava Panikkar (3 June 1895 – 10 December 1963) was an historian and diplomat. Educated in Madras and University of Oxford (1914), he read for the Bar at Middle Temple in London. Returning to India, he was a Professor at Aligarh Muslim University's off centre campus in Bengal before becoming editor of the *Hindustan Times* in 1925. He then served as Foreign Minister for the State of Patiala and then became Prime Minister of Bikaner. Panikkar represented India at the 1947 session of the UN General Assembly. In 1950, he was appointed India's first ambassador to China and later as envoy to Egypt in 1952. He was also India's ambassador to France and a member of the Rajya Sabha (upper house of Parliament).

2 Sahodaran Aiyappan was one of the founders of the trade union movement in Kerala. In 1928, Ayyappan was elected to Cochin Legislative Council of which he continued to be a member for the next 21 years, also serving as a Cabinet minister. Aiyappan was an atheist although he was close to Sree Narayana Guru, the reformist leader of the *Ezhava* community.

3 T. Komalezhathu Madhavan (2 September 1885 – 27 April 1930) was a social reformer from the *Ezhava* community involved with Sree Narayana Dharma Paripalana Sangham. He fought against the practise of untouchability and was a leader of the Temple Entry protest at Vaikom.

4 Erode Venkatappa Ramasamy (17 September 1879 – 24 December 1973) was a fiery Tamil activist who questioned the Brahmin domination of social, cultural and political life in southern India at the time. He was head of the Justice Party in 1939 and changed its name to Dravida Kazhagam in 1944 and began espousing the cause of an independent Dravida Nadu, based on Tamil language and culture. The present day Dravida Munnetra Kazhagam, the Anna Dravida Munnetra Kazhagam and various other smaller parties in present day Tamil Nadu are offshoots of the DK.

When the effects of the Great Depression (1929 to 1939) hit Cochin, Salem was at the forefront of labour politics and doing pioneering work in pushing for workers' rights. He was one of the founders of the Cochin Port Labour Association in 1928[5].

In 1930, he was appointed to handle negotiations with the port management on issues related to lightermen and other labourers who struck work demanding higher wages.[6] The same year he was also named president of a new Cochin Labour Association - while involved in a strike of workers in a coir factory. The strike failed.[7]

Salem was involved in political work at this time - partly to get away from acrimonious synagogue politics - and was a participant at the All-India States' Subjects Conference and the session of the Indian National Congress in Madras in December 1927. Soon after his return to Cochin, he was active in the first Kerala State Subjects Conference in Ernakulam, chaired by R. K. Shanmukham Chetty.[8]

In 1929, he became one of the powerful secretaries of the Indian States' Peoples Party formed during the Lahore[9] Congress session of the Indian National Congress, chaired by Jawaharlal Nehru. The group represented Congressmen from the princely states. On December 31, 1929, Nehru hoisted the Indian tricolour on the banks of the Ravi River in Lahore. Salem was among those who read aloud the Pledge of Independence. The Lahore session also requested Mahatma Gandhi to lead the Civil Disobedience

---

5 Cited by Prof. Chiriyankandath - *from K. P. Kannan, Of rural proletarian struggles: mobilization and organization of rural workers in Southwest India, Delhi: Oxford University Press, 1988, pg 30.*

6 Ibid, *Madras Mail of 4 April, 1930, pg 30.*

7 Ibid, *Madras Mail, 18 and 26 June and 20 July, 1931; JLMM, A. B. Salem's diary for 1930-1, entry for 18 June 1931, pg 31.*

8 Sir Ramasamy Chetty Kandasamy Shanmukham Chetty KCIE (1892 – 1953), a wealthy industrialist/banker and lawyer, served as independent India's first finance minister from 1947 to 1949. He was also President of India's Central Legislative Assembly from 1933 to 1935 as a member of the Swarajya Party and Diwan of the Cochin Kingdom from 1935 to 1941. The most prominent thoroughfare in Kochi today is known as Shanmukham Road.

9 Lahore became a Pakistani city after the partition of India in 1947. It is located about 56 km from the Indian border.

Movement. Soon afterwards, 172 members of the central and provincial legislatures in British India resigned from their posts to begin a massive non-violent national revolt against colonial rule. The Declaration of Independence (call for *Poorna Swaraj* - *poorna* means complete/full/total and *Swaraj* is self-rule in Sanskrit) was promulgated by the Congress Party on January 26, 1930.[10]

In 1929, the South Indian States' Peoples Conference was held under the auspices of the Travancore State People's Committee at Trivandrum, under the chairmanship of Sir Viswesarayya,[11] which gave an impetus to political personalities from southern India to enter the national movement.

The next year at the People's Party Conference in Bangalore, Salem introduced a resolution calling for total independence for India from colonial rule (mirroring the *Poorna Swaraj* call adopted at the Lahore session). The conference also passed another resolution calling for the setting up of governments with parliamentary accountability in the princely states with immediate effect.[12]

In 1930, he was almost certain to be arrested in the neighbouring Kingdom of Travancore, when he made speeches in the Alleppey region about temperance and alcohol abstinence along with remarks about the ongoing temple entry movement for the lower castes of Hindu society. He was identified as a trouble maker by a local Travancore magistrate and banned from speaking in the area. Always a man to follow the law, Salem did not defy the order and returned quickly to Cochin.[13]

Salem first won election in 1925 to the new Cochin Council

10 January 26 is celebrated today as India's Republic Day. It was also the day that the Indian Constitution came into effect - January 26, 1950.

11 Sir Mokshagundam Visvesvaraya (1861-1962) was a civil engineer who became Diwan of Mysore Princely State (1912-1919). Several metro stations, universities, technical colleges and institutes have been named after him. He designed and built the famous Krishna Raja Sagar Dam. Along with several honours given by the British Empire, he was also one of the earliest recipients of the Bharat Ratna, India's highest civilian award - in 1955. His birthday on September 15 is celebrated as Engineers's Day in India.

12 Cited by Prof. Chiriyankandath - from *Madras Mail*, 1 and 2 September 1930; JLMM, *A. B. Salem's diary for 1930-1*, entries for 31 August and 1 September, 1930, pg 31.

13 Cited by Prof. Chiriyankandath, JLMM, *A. B. Salem's diary for 1930-1*, entry for 21 September, 1930.

from the Special Jewish Constituency, when Samuel S. Koder (1869–1941) vacated his seat after winning the election from the open Mattancherry constituency.

Koder was one of Cochin's wealthiest businessmen and warden of the Paradesi synagogue. Salem was one of his business associates in various ventures, including the Cochin Electric Company and the Cochin Ferry.

Koder won the election in Mattancherry with the support of another famous figure in the region's history, Popatlal Govardhan Lalan, a wealthy Gujarati merchant.[14]

During the following term, Popatlal contested the open seat in Mattancherry while Koder claimed the special Jewish seat. Salem lost out to Popatlal Lalan by a margin of over 400 votes, a shameful drubbing, considering the number of voters in the constituency.[15]

Salem couldn't believe that he could lose his Mattancherry seat. He alleged foul play and lodged a complaint with the Ernakulam District Magistrate's court charging that Lalan and his allies who were members of the Mattancherry municipal council, had not allowed Salem and his supporters to cast their votes. He lost the case. Lalan was elected to the Cochin Legislative Assembly for three successive terms. The Gujaratis, like the Paradesi Jews, came to Cochin in the 1500s and it is estimated that there were about 700 families in Mattancherry - enough to swing votes for members of their community. They had a community organization called the Shri Cochin Gujarati Mahajan which was founded in 1893 and is active even today.

Two months later, Salem stood for election again in an open constituency by-election from the town of Chalakudy in Trichur

---

14 Popatlal Govardhan Lalan, who was appointed an Honorary Magistrate at the age of 24, was the founder of the renowned Indo-Mercantile Bank which was acquired by the State Bank of Travancore in 1959. Lalan was responsible for ending animal sacrifices at many Hindu temples in Cochin. His family built the Chandraprabha Temple and he was also instrumental in building the Cochin Jain Temple. Lalan served as President of the Indian Chamber of Commerce in Cochin and died while he was chairman of the Mattancherry Municipal Council. There is a Lalan Road, adjacent to the Thekkemadam Dharma Shasta temple in Mattancherry.

15 Cited by Prof. Chiriyankandath - JLMM, *A. B. Salem's diary for 1930-1*, entry for 23 May, 1931; T. Jamal Mohamed, *The Gujaratis: a study of socio-economic interactions [1850-1950]*, Delhi: Deputy Publications, 1990, pg. 175.

district where he was defeated by a wealthy Syrian Christian businessman named A. I. Mani. He wrote in his diary: 'Such is the end of two contests in the election of 1106 [Malayalam Era] to the Cochin Legislative Council. The lack of money is the cause & nothing else!'[16]

He was obliquely referring to S. S. Koder and other Jews of the Paradesi community who didn't back him for the seat. Most of them also did not have a favourable view of his nationalist leanings and anti-imperialist, anti-monarchist stand.

He took an active interest, however, in the proceedings of the assembly, even writing letters to the Progressive Party's assembly leader Dr. A. G. Menon, making suggestions about campaigning for more responsible government.[17]

At about this time, several new political groupings began to gain strength in the kingdom. These included the Cochin Congress, Cochin State Congress, Unionist Party, Progressive Party, The Democratic Party and units of communist and socialist-oriented parties, each with their own firebrand leaders.

He used this period in the political wilderness to study about Zionism - and in 1933 visited Palestine where he stayed for five months, which turned him into an ardent Zionist as well.

Salem got his second chance to serve in the Legislative Council again from 1939 to 1945. The elder S. S. Koder's son, 35-year-old university graduate Shabtai Samuel Koder, who was now managing the immense wealth of the Koder family, was the Jewish representative on the council,"[18] while Salem won the election in the open Mattancherry seat.

However, unlike in 1931, the entire Jewish community and the merchant class of the region voted en bloc for Salem, especially after the elder Koder made exhortations in the synagogue and outside to garner support for Salem.

---

16 Cited by Prof. Chiriyankandath - *JLMM, A. B. Salem's diary for 1930–1, entry for 20 May, 1931*, pg 33.

17 Cited by Prof. Chiriyankandath, *JLMM, A. B. Salem's diary for 1930–1, entries for 2 and 4 August 1931*; *Madras Mail,* 15 December, 1932, pg 3.

18 *The Chicago Sentinel,* 25, November, 1937 - digital version (National Library of Israel.)

(It was during this term in the Cochin Legislative Council, that the then Diwan of Cochin, Shanmukham Chetty - with whom A. B. Salem had a warm relationship - had expressed an interest in establishing trade connections between Cochin and the Jewish Agency of Palestine.[19])

Salem's second tenure in parliamentary politics was, however, considerably mellow when compared with his first. A lot of the fire within him had died down - mainly because other younger, radical leaders had risen from working class ranks to control the left movement.

"The younger generation of political activists regarded him as a marginal and idiosyncratic figure from the past, prone to giving humorous speeches about local politics in his strongly accented Malayalam on Salem's Hill or from a rickshaw travelling about town."[20]

When he stood for election again - this time from the open Njarakkal constituency in Ernakulam district, he suffered a humiliating defeat, bagging only 36 votes, from over 1,700 that were cast mostly by Catholic voters.

Some years earlier, in 1937, a committee of the Cochin Government had recommended the scrapping of the special Jewish seat in the legislative council, much to the chagrin of the Jews in Mattancherry and Ernakulam. The committee said the 'small Jewish population of about 1,451 people in the total population of over 1,205,016 did not warrant its continuance.'[21]

The government, however, continued to nominate a Jewish member to the council until 1949 when the new Tiru-Cochin state was formed after India's independence and the Maharaja relinquished his rule. The South Indian Jewish Association sent several memorandums to the ruling establishment and to the federal government about how the Jews had been relegated to the bottom rungs of social and political life.

---

19 Kumaraswamy, P. R. *India's Israel Policy*, Columbia University Press, New York, 2010.

20 Prof. Chiriyankandath - interview with an Ernakulam Congress worker, Cited in *'Nationalism, religion and community...'* Journal of Global History, pg 34.

21 *The Jewish Daily Bulletin*, November 7, 1937, Jewish Telegraphic Agency Archives.

Although Salem's fight for responsible government came to fruition after India attained Independence, he failed again to win a seat in the first election based on universal adult franchise held in Cochin - although his party won with an overwhelming mandate. The Jewish nominated seat was also abolished.

His final bid to continue in electoral politics in a free India ended after he stood as a Congress candidate in the Mattancherry municipal elections in 1956. He was defeated by a Communist Party worker. The Congress party soon began to ignore him and most links were loosened after he declined to attend and address an important political conference during Rosh Hashanah celebrations. Instead, he opted to stay in the synagogue.

Even so, he continued writing letters to national leaders and others putting forth his political ideas, mainly on India-Israel relations. His political activities came to a full end after he suffered a stroke in 1959 and was confined to a wheelchair.

Some of Salem's contemporaries and associates went on to become ministers in the Kerala government in later years, notching up electoral victories in assembly elections. They included Dr. A. R. Menon, a former physician, who became the first Minister for Health in the new state of Kerala. Menon served as a member of the Cochin Legislative Council from 1925 to 1945 (along with Salem during two terms).

Another was K. T. Achutan, advocate and senior Congress leader, who served in both the Kochi Legislative Assembly and Travancore-Cochin Legislative Assembly. He was also elected to the Indian parliament in 1952.

M. K. Raghavan, a successful lawyer and Congress leader, a founding member of the Cochin Port and Dock Workers Union and chairman of Mattancheri Municipal Council (Salem's area of influence), was twice elected to the Kerala assembly and served as Minister of Labour and Housing.

There were many others who became well-known names in Kerala politics - as Salem faded from the scene.

•••••

After India became independent, Maulana Abul Kalam Azad had emerged as Prime Minister Jawaharal Nehru's principal advisor on Middle East policy and, according to Michael Brecher, sabotaged Nehru's plans to normalize relations with Israel in 1952.[22]

Journalist T. V. R. Shenoy also wrote: "Pandit Nehru - reputedly under Maulana Azad's influence - refused to have diplomatic relations with the Jewish State. There would be no Indian embassy in Israel until a quarter of a century after Salem's death, more than four decades of wasted diplomatic opportunity."[23]

(Maulana Abul Kalam Azad - Sayyid Ghulam Muhiyuddin Ahmed bin Khairuddin Al Hussaini - was independent India's first Minister of Education. He was one of the leaders of the Khilafat Movement, a pan-Islamic protest campaign in the 1920s to save the Ottoman Caliphate. In 1924, however, Turkey abolished the Caliphate.)

This move by Azad had repercussions in Cochin because in opposing ties with Israel, he also put a stop to Salem's bid to become the first Indian envoy to the Jewish state, a post which he yearned for, especially since he had established a good rapport with the Israeli leadership. His petition in this regard was not heeded and this put off Salem so much that he decided not to have anything to do with the government in New Delhi.

"While Salem's talents as an orator and as an organizer were welcome in the days of the Raj, his influence rapidly waned when politics became a numbers game. Simply put, there weren't enough Jews to give Salem a solid electoral foundation".[24]

"It was this Maulana Azad who was close to Nehru in those days... He did not like my father's proposal that he be sent to Israel... Actually, Maulana did not like my father. So Nehru said 'no'".[25]

Nehru was, however, keen to keep Salem within his circle. According to Gumliel Salem: "I remember how one early morning, somebody came rushing to our home saying an emissary had

22 Kumaraswamy P. R., *India's Israel Policy*, Columbia University Press, New York, 2010, pg 63. Michael Brecher is a polticial scientist in Montreal who wrote a scholarly book *Nehru: A Political Biography* in 1959.

23 Shenoy, T. V. R. *The Jewish Gandhi and Barack Obama*, Sept. 08, 2008, rediff.com

24 Ibid.

25 Gumliel Salem, personal conversation, 2015.

arrived from Delhi to Mattancherry and had entered Jew Town with a message from Prime Minister Nehru.

"Dad dressed quickly and went to hide in the synagogue. He did not want to meet the messenger. He sat in the synagogue for most of the day. Later, we heard that Prime Minister Nehru wanted to offer him some sort of ministerial rank or advisory post in his government.

"All of us in the community felt that he should have taken up the offer and gone to Delhi. Instead, he wasted his immense talent in this tiny corner of the world, and focused only on the synagogue; that was his world at that moment. It was ridiculous and it was disappointing. I have not forgiven him for his lapse of reasoning to this day."[26]

26 Ibid.

CHAPTER VII

Salem In Cochin Council

In 1913, the Maharaja of Cochin had first declared the need for some sort of advisory body to gauge public opinion on various issues and in 1923, the Maharaja promulgated the Cochin Legislative Council Regulation.

The following year, A. B. Salem published a revolutionary pamphlet demanding 'responsible government' in the Cochin Kingdom. The idea was far-fetched but it attracted the attention of the Maharaja and senior members of his court.[1]

The Cochin Legislative Council was formally established In the summer of 1925 (April 3), in the Maharaja's official residence of Hill palace in Thrippunithura.

It was a far-reaching decision and one of the founding stones of parliamentary democracy in India. Membership in the Council was "based upon property and allied qualifications. Besides general constituencies, certain special constituencies were created to represent interests such as those of landlords and planters."[2]

---

1 Abraham B. Salem, *Cochin political pamphlet No. 1: A scheme for a constitution in Cochin*, Ernakulam, 1924 - Cited by Chiriyankandath - from reports in the *Madras Mail*.

2 History of legislative bodies in Kerala - Cochin Council
http://keralaassembly.org/history/cochin.html

A. B. Salem was elected to the Council as a special representative of the Jewish community in the Kingdom of Cochin.

The Council was given the authority to introduce a limited number of public interest bills, ask for specific information from the government on various administrative issues, move resolutions and to discuss and vote on budget demands.

The first president of the assembly was T. S. Narayana Aiyer and in 1926 two select committees were formed. In 1935, four additional Standing Advisory Committees were constituted. Cochin also became the first among Indian princely states to appoint a Minister from the elected members, after a system of diarchy was introduced in 1938 under the Government of Cochin Act

Ambat Sivarama Menon was chosen as Minister for Rural Development. Gradually, several powers were handed over to the assembly until 1948 when full adult franchise was introduced and the first popularly elected government, headed by Ikkanda Warrier was formed on September 20, 1948. It remained in office until the integration of Travancore and Cochin on July 1, 1949, as Tiru-Cochi state.

•••••

Soon after his appointment to the Council, Salem drafted a constitution that was signed by 28 of the 30 members of the house. The document was presented to the then Diwan of Cochin T. A. Narayana Aiyer, who simply filed it away.[3]

Salem did not give up. Within six months of drafting the constitution, he had become a member of a caucus in the assembly which called itself the Progressive Party and became the party Whip - in a bid to force the government to set up some sort of responsible government.[4]

In 1930, Salem and other members of the assembly demanded an Act defining the government responsibilities, an Executive

---

3 Rao Bahadur Tarakat Subramania Narayana Aiyer (born October 1898) was a lawyer, civil servant and administrator who served as the Diwan of the Cochin kingdom from 1925 to 1930. He served as Chief Justice of the Cochin Court before being appointed Diwan. He played a vital role in the construction of water pipelines to Trichur, Mattancheri, Nemmara and Ayalore.

4 As per reports in the Madras Mail of August 5, 1926, and March 1, 1927. Cited by Chiriyankandath.

Council, an elected deputy president and the right of members to ask supplementary questions along with other powers. To press their point, they also rejected the required budget appropriations of various departments.

The Diwan overrode their actions and opined that any constitutional reforms should be slow and called upon the members to 'give up pursuing a dubious and thorny path' that led nowhere. [5]

He added: "...constitutional reform is a plant of very slow and steady growth and you cannot expect it to became a fully developed tree in course of a year or even a decade."[6]

The Diwan was replaced in December 1930 by a British officer C. C. Herbert (1930-1935) whom Salem supported and described as a 'firm and matter of fact man' and Salem suspended his intransigent behaviour. [7]

'[Diwan Herbert's] good Judgment, ability, industry and sympathy have made a very great impression on the vast majority of the people of Cochin who undoubtedly have complete confidence in him. Were he to leave, I do not imagine that we would find another suitable European I. C. S. Officer... with Herbert's conscience and self-respect..."[8] (ICS - Indian Civil Service).

A. B. Salem often lambasted the British in political forums and in his street speeches. Decades before the notion of full independence became part of the Indian political psyche, in his limited role as a representative in the Cochin Legislative Council, he thundered against the injustice of being ruled by foreigners.

"We have to satisfy the British Indian Government in India. It is called the Indian Government; it would have been much better styled "the British Indian Government in India". These words often invited adverse comments in the council and caused uneasiness in senior levels of Government, and among the wealthy class who feared it would invite retribution.

5 As per report in the *Madras Mail,* August 18, 1930, cited by Chiriyankandath.

6 Diwan's letter to council members, August 15, 1930.

7 *Salem Diary* - entry for December 1, 1930, cited by Chiriyankandath.

8 Letter by Lt. Colonel. H. R. N. Pritchard C.I.E., C.B.E. Agent to the Governor-General to ir Charles Watson, Political Secretary to the Government of India on January 3, 1932. *www.cochinroyalhistory.org*

••••

A. B. Salem made several remarkable speeches in the Cochin Legislature. All his pronouncements on diverse subjects made in the early 20th century remain socially and politically relevant even today.

Long before the concept of social welfare and compassion towards socially and financially disparate elements of society became part of Liberal ideology in the west, Salem formulated and gave concrete form to the idea of a welfare structure in 1926, in the nascent legislature of the Cochin kingdom.

His introduction of the Salem Cochin Old Age and Widows' Relief bill is a piece of reform legislation that influenced laws during the following decades in all parts of India.

In addition, he also pioneered the discussion and passage of several important pieces of legislation, including:

On the Question of Retaining English as the Official language;

The Question of Hoarding and Profiteering;

The Question of Visitor Comfort at Government Offices;

The Question of Sacking Old Employees and Getting New Ones;

The Question of Water Supply and Other Essential Services;

And much more...

Salem had total command of the English language and his speeches in the council were well-articulated, forceful and logical, often generating laughter and applause because of his acerbic tongue and choice of words.

To give an example: "...having heard the very beautiful, eloquent and diplomatic statement of the Revenue Member, I rise to congratulate him as the best charming player on the harp of the Government. Shall I characterize his statement as the best piece of official hypocrisy, and if that be a strong word, I would say his was a diplomatic way of putting things..."

ABRAHAM BARAK SALEM'S COCHIN OLD AGE AND WIDOWS' RELIEF BILL

(Minutes prepared by T.K. Krishna Menon, Secretary to the Council)

Salem introduced the bill in the Legislative Council on February 1, 1926.

A. B. Salem: Sir, I beg leave to have [this] adjourned to a subsequent meeting, because I have asked the Government for certain statements as regards the number of persons that would come under the category of persons entitled to these pensions. The Government, I understand, is collecting the necessary statistics, and as there is no great hurry to rush through this Bill, I pray that you would be pleased to adjourn this to a subsequent meeting, and allow me to move it then, after obtaining the statistics from the Government.

The council president pointed out that the bills would lapse if they are not read in Council.

A. B. Salem: So I can have it held over for two sessions. I can adjourn it for two sessions, but not more, so that at the next session, I can have it introduced. On the termination of the session, all pending notices shall lapse and fresh notices will have to be served for the next session.

•••••

February 1, 1926 -

On expenditure in schools:

A. B. Salem: What amount of money is spent upon the non-depressed classes on an average?

C. Mathai: I said in the same school all sorts of pupils are taught. We have thrown open our schools even to the most depressed classes, and we find caste-Hindus, Christians, Muhammadans, *Pulayas*[9] and others, sitting side by side.

A. B. Salem: My question is what is the average expenditure spent on a child?

C. Mathai: ...I am not quite sure. It is about Rs. 6, I think.

A. B. Salem: Sir, I find that there is no difficulty for the Government to accept this resolution.

I do not think I am betraying the confidence of the mover when I say that this resolution was hatched in consultation with the speaker himself.

We were for introducing Free and Compulsory Primary educa-

---

9 The *Pulayas* or soil slaves were agricultural labourers at the lowest rung of Kerala society during the Middle Ages right until the 20th century. Today, they have an organization called Kerala Pulaya Maha Sabha (KPMS) and are politically strong and upwardly mobile socially and economically.

tion throughout the State. We went into the matter and found, as the Director of Public Instruction has pointed out, that free compulsory education for the whole State is absolutely unnecessary, and we congratulated ourselves upon the position Cochin has attained in India in the matter of education and literacy.

Sir, when we have for every square mile a school (as we have 780 institutions in 821 square miles, and when we have nearly 10 per cent of the population in schools - to be exact, 97,043 out of 900,000 of population are in schools - and when we have such a state of affairs, it is unnecessary to ask for compulsory education, and I perfectly agree with he department and I congratulate the Hon'ble Member upon his advice to avoid compulsion in general.

Now, Sir, I find that the depressed classes of the so-called depressed classes are very small in number. We would be glad to omit the word 'Thiyyas'[10] from the resolution, and I confine my remarks on the resolution only to the depressed classes, of whom we have only 15,000 pupils, who can be brought into schools by compulsion. If I have understood the Director of Public Instruction correctly, for these 15,000 pupils of the depressed classes, his estimate is 6 lakhs of rupees. That means Rs. 40 a child, which, I say, is 8 times more than what the department is spending upon any other child.

C. Mathai: What about feeding?

A. B. Salem: We are not asking you to feed the children of the depressed classes. We have got 10 per cent of the depressed classes in schools and want the Government to take steps to bring the remaining 90 per cent into the fold of knowledge. We want to bring them into the orbit of education and instruction. We want particularly *Pulayas* and *Nayadis*[11] - who are without instructions - to be brought into schools and instructed.

We ask only for compulsion with respect to this particular class, because for various reasons of suppression, depression, oppression, they are out of the pale of culture and civilization. To atone for their suppressed and depressed condition, we must elevate them, as we have elevated others, by bringing them within

10 *Thiyyas* - a prominent Hindu caste group, mostly in northern Kerala.

11 *Nayadis* - once an oppressed group in the Hindu caste system of south India.

the light of instruction, so that they may carry a little light to their dark homes.

President: Without feeding them, can we induce them to come into schools?

A. B. Salem: I say, Sir, if you give Re. 1 to every child for coming to school a month, we have only to spend Rs. 15,000 a month and that will be a very large amount. But even 8 *annas*[12] is sufficient in my view.

C. Matthai: Will the Hon'ble Member guarantee?

A. B. Salem: It is only an experiment worth trying.

C. Matthai: Every week we give a hearty meal and still they disappear.

A. B. Salem: Much of the money was actually misappropriated.

C. Matthai: In places where it was not misappropriated, the very same thing happened....One meal on every Friday [will] cost 1 anna and 3 pies.

President: So, for one month, it will be only 5 *annas*. Mr. Salem wants it raised to Re. 1.

C. Matthai: And that to be given in coin.

A. B. Salem: I am only suggesting one idea. There are only 15,000 children amidst these classes. For these, the Director wants 6 lakhs or Rs. 40 a year on a child. It is a very, very high figure. Spend Rs. 6, 7 or Rs. 10 on a child, and then it will be only 1 1/4 lakhs.

C. Matthai: Not only feeding. We want teachers, buildings, etc and all that comes to a big amount.

A. B. Salem: [Building as a capital expenditure] is not to be regarded as an expenditure in this case. Who wants buildings for these depressed classes? (*Legislators shout: Hear, Hear*), They can sit under a banyan tree.

C. Matthai: What will they do during the heavy monsoon?

A. B. Salem: Give two months' holiday at that time.

•••••

A. B. Salem: What I may suggest is that an attempt be made to start with Re. 1 a pupil, and I suggest that a lakh may be earmarked for a few years, say 6 years and thus make an attempt toward the

---

12 *Anna* was a currency unit formerly used throughout India, equal to 1/16 of Rupee.

elevation of the so-called depressed classes.

A member named **K. T. Mathew** *interjects: The amount of Re. 1 may be used by the elders of the family for drinking.*

C. Matthai: Now, I remember an instance. In Chalakudy, I asked a child why he did not go to school. He told me that he had no clothes. Then I asked him whether the Headmaster had given him clothes The child told me that the clothes were appropriated by the elders. So I have now given shirts, which I believe the elders will not appropriate, since they will not fit them. (*Laughter*).

A. B. Salem: So my humble submission is that without compulsion it is not possible to bring these [pupils] in. But the Government can keep this resolution in view, and earmark a sum of money for the specific purpose of imparting some sort of instruction to these so-called depressed classes, so that light and learning may penetrate their homes.

House adjourns after the president rules there was no amendment needed as Salem was 'not for compulsion and was only emphasizing financial considerations.'

•••••

Raising a legal issue during a discussion of the Municipal Regulation Amendment Bill. February 3, 1926. A. B. Salem's argumentative nature comes to fore in this exchange with the President of the council:

A. B. Salem: I wish to raise a point of order, Sir. The complete deletion of a clause will not be considered as an amendment. It has been ruled so on a previous occasion.

President: But Mr. Salem, there were two clauses relating to two distinct matters. The Government may accept the amendment.

A. B. Salem: That the Government may do. Is it not proper for the Government to go by way of an amendment of the bill itself?

President: When one section or one clause in which the whole principle is involved is sought to be deleted, the whole bill goes. But here the principle of the whole bill is not negatived. I can allow the amendment. Here there are two clauses. But the deletion of one of them, the principle of the whole bill is not negatived.

A. B. Salem: When I proposed an amendment to the Chief Court

Regulation Amendment Bill - that Rs. 3,000 should be changed to Rs 2,000 as the limit - you ruled that the amendment would be negativing the whole bill, and that it would not come to an amendment, and it was ruled that it was out of order altogether, although the amendment was proposed and seconded.

The objection was that it cut at the root of the section altogether and so it could not be moved as an amendment at all. The only procedure that we could then find out from the Standing Order is that, when a clause is read, and if we oppose it, we can simply say we could not pass that. So it would not be an amendment when the whole clause is sought to be deleted. Then there is nothing to amend. It will not be an amendment to the particular clause for the whole clause is deleted.

The discussion continues...

A. B. Salem: I think it was ruled the other day the deletion of a clause would come to an amendment. There were two clauses in the Chief Court Regulation Amendment Bill. When I brought in an amendment to delete one clause out of that Regulation, it was not considered to be an amendment.

Other members intervene with their comments...

•••••

DISCUSSION ON EXTENSION OF TERM
FOR MUNICIPAL CHAIRMAN.

Salem wanted the term to be fixed at two years so that the council 'need not endure the term of an unwelcome chairman who sticks on to his vested rights.' A very interesting observation indeed that is relevant in today's Indian politics!

A. B. Salem: Sir, I rise to support the amendment and to oppose the extension of the period of the Chairman to three years. The argument brought forward is that it will take one year at least for a Chairman to understand the work of the office and the Municipal administration, to understand the rottenness of the machinery, and so on.

At the same time, Sir, I cannot forget the fact that the Chairman may come to the Municipality with a very small majority and he may have a very hard time in the Council. We have had such experience in the Mattancherry Council.

Sometimes a Chairman who is not pleasing to the Council is elected. He has his vested rights. He may stick on to the vested rights, in spite of the fact that censure motions are passed. In that case, the sooner the Chairman;' term ends, the better for all.

So that aspect of the question must be lost sight of. The Council should not be forced to endure with the tern of an unwelcome Chairman for a longer period than they generally have to. Now, by extending the term, such a contingency may also arise. Only one Council has sat under the new Regulation, and the second Council is only coming into existence.

It is too premature for us to say that any particular scheme that has been enunciated or initiated by a particular Chairman has not been carried out. We have not heard any member, nether the mover nor the supporter, state any particular scheme which a particular Chairman has initiated and which he could not successfully leave to his successor to deal with.

Sir, if a Chairman with good qualities, as mentioned by the Hon'ble Member from Irinjalakuda, exercises his function to the satisfaction of the members of the Council, what would be the result? Hew would be certainly re-elected with greater honour to carry out the scheme.

I certainly ask the Chairman to stand upon the judgement of the voters than upon the power conferred upon them. If, upon their goodwill, a Chairman is returned time after time, there will be a greater honour to him than to stick to his appointment like a leech for three years, even when he is not wanted.

There would be difficulties coming in the way if we extend the term. We had one particular instance in Mattancherry Town. The Hon'ble Member for Irinjalakuda said that in his Council they moved in perfect unison, because they all agree to fight with the Government. That was their policy.

Dr. A. R. Menon: That is not what I said.

A. B. Salem: I shall refer to his speech. I will not make any statement of which I am not sure of (*Laughter*). These must also be considered when we take the provisions of the amendment into consideration. I think it is too soon to amend the Regulation of

1096. This is not the last word that is to be said in the matter.

There has not been any report by the Government or the controlling authorities to the effect that schemes initiated by the Chairman are not coming to fruition because of the shortness of time. After all, what are the schemes that the Municipality can have, excepting a water supply scheme, which they will not be able to carry out?

Other schemes that they have to initiate are all in the Municipal Regulations. The Municipal Regulation lays down the scope of their activities, and those activities certainly do not require three years to carry out.

They have to burn the rubbish from the roads, etc. In the matter of constructing roads, they have not much to do for three years. Even if not completed, the alignment is there, and the sanctioned money also will come, whoever be the Chairman. What is the other great scheme that the Municipality has to initiate in three years' time?

This extension of time has also another defect. It will curtail the rights of the voters. Many a voter may have an idea of becoming a Chairman.

We must give them also as many chances as possible to come up and do what they can in the Municipality. So if you extend the term of the Chairman, the chances of others will be limited. I would like to have the period reduced to one year, because we know that even in big cities in Europe and America, Governments fall within few months of office - sometimes in a few days - after they come into power.

In these days, in a self-governing institution, I think it should not be advisable to extend the term. In my humble view, an extension of the term of a Chairman to three years is not necessary.

(A. B. Salem was on the losing side of the vote 23-4 and the Council decided to extend the term of the Chairman to three years.)

DEBATE ON MALAYALAM IN GOVERNMENT OFFICES AND COURTS - FEBRUARY 3, 1926

A. B. Salem was an ardent proponent of the English language and wanted it to be the official language in the Kingdom and it was also part of his vision for a future India. He declared: "From the Himalayas to Cape Comorin, the only language that is possible, which will unite us into one nation, which will not isolate us (there is only one language possible even today) and that language is the English language."

A. B. Salem: Sir, I rise to oppose the resolution. It is with deep regret that I have to be told that I am not national in opposing this resolution. But nationality, to be sound, must have a value. Whether, by debating this resolution, we will strengthen ourselves or weaken ourselves is the question. Sir, the world has become very small, thanks to the transport facilities, to the wireless, to the telegraph, and in the quick means of communication that take you around the world in 80 days, as it were.

Now, Sir, in the olden days when it took three days to reach Shornur from Ernakulam, it was well and good to say that we could carry out all our work in the vernacular. We were then an isolated part of the world, cut away by water and the difficulties of communications from the outside world.

But today, the conditions are absolutely different. We have in front of us the Harbour coming, and that will bring the whole world into our midst soon. And then, what are we to do with the vernacular alone? That is the point.

Then, Sir, in these days of progress in transport, you will get the same speed, if you put your work in the vernacular, as you will get in these days of motor cars if you still want to travel out of patriotic motives in carts drawn by bullocks. I imagine, Sir, patriotic gentlemen rising up and saying that, in these days, when our money is being drained, we should not travel in foreign motorcars, and that it is absolutely irrational and non-national to use motor cars, and pressing us to go back to the days of bullock carts and then see how many members of this House would subscribe to that proposition.

In the same way, Sir, our vernacular will only be useful in this one district of Kerala. I say the word 'Kerala', because from Gokarnam to Cape Comorin you may go on with vernacular, but if you will cross the boundary into Coimbatore or into the Chittur Taluk of the Cochin State itself, you will find that this vernacular will be of no material use to you.

What will be the result of vernacularization, Sir? Unemployment will result. A man may want a clerk who should type a few letters and attend to his correspondence. Suppose you have only vernacular established. Suppose that a poor young man, after all his education in the country in the vernacular, seeks an employment. He would get no employment in any house that has communications with the world. Patriotic men, patriotic landholders may employ him, but they will be able to give him only a pittance. Therefore, the economic value of the vernacular is gone.

Sir, some years ago, this controversy was raised in the Legislative Council of Madras. At the time, seeing one of the Hon'ble Members there standing out for vernacular, I wrote an article upon vernacular education in the "Common Weal"[13], which is no longer in existence. (*Laughter*).

In that article, I pointed out how the Hon'ble Member was short-sighted to stand up for the vernacular, because as, I said, in Madras, there were not less than four main vernaculars. Now if the country is to be united, it must have one language. From the Himalayas to Cape Comorin, the only language that is possible, which will unite us into one nation, which will not isolate us (there is only one language possible even today)' and that language is the English language.

So long as we are destined to be within this Empire, we must have one common language, one common aspiration and one common object and that can only be attained by an exchange of ideas between the various component peoples of the Empire.

How on earth can we communicate to one another and to get rid of angularities and bring about a great brotherhood of humanity within the Empire, unless we have one common language?

Therefore, Sir, to go back to the days of the vernacular would be a highly detrimental work. It will reflect not progress but retrogression. It will lead us back to the bullock cart days in these days of motor cars and the progress will be as slow. We will have to go

---

13 '*Common Weal*' was a newspaper founded in Madras in 1914 by theosophist and activist Annie Besant. She was also a founder of Benares Hindu University and an active member of the Indian National Congress.

back and come forward again.

I know how many hours I had to study vernacular for the B.A. Degree examination, and after all, of what use it is to me? It is of no use to me at all. Even here in Cochin, it is of very little use except for political meetings outside. (*Laughter*).

It is only where we have to address the masses that we have to use the vernacular. The masses everywhere will not be able to go beyond the vernacular.

Now, Sir, there is a great misapprehension that it is the masses that have to be thought of. There is no country in the world that the masses rule. It is always the classes that rule. And if the classes are drawn from the masses, and if they are all one or won, then one portion of the masses become the classes. Because of the fact that we talk and teach not in the vernacular, but in the language of the Empire, it does not follow that we are unpatriotic.

Sir, we have been referred to many points by the Hon'ble mover. He said that English is foreign in character. Certainly not, in these days. A time there was when English was foreign. Now after 150 years of British sway, we have begun to think - thinking operations have begun - and the political classes, particularly, have begun to think, in English at this time. And if we are to progress politically, and to battle with the most highly politically developed people, we can do that only be mastering that language and familiarizing our ideas also in that language.

Again, Sir, it was said that the language of the ruler and the ruled must be one. Sir, in that I perfectly agree. After all, Sir, when everything is said and done, we are ruled in this Empire by the predominant partner - I say the "predominant partner", because the old ideas of dominance is being gradually given up.

The idea of partnership is coming, and the predominant partner rules and sways, and therefore, the language of the Ruler and the ruled must gradually become one and the same. I wish every child is taught English as well as the vernacular. The vernacular will do for his local needs and the English for his higher needs.

Again, Sir, the argument that 90 per cent speak only the vernacular is no argument to say that all that takes place in the Government should be in the vernacular. Sir, what takes place in the

Government is equally for this State as well as for other parts of India and the predominant partner. We have to satisfy the British Indian Government in India. It is called the Indian Government; it would have been much better styled "the British Indian Government in India".

Therefore, Sir, for those politically highly placed people, to understand what we are doing here, and what we are doing in the state, it will be easier, it will be much more economical, to have English the language in which all the important transactions that take place.

Sir, I may tell the Hon'ble mover that every judgment of the Chief Court, when dealing with the life of a person, if it is a sentence of death, every bit of the proceedings, has to be translated into the English language. That is the condition of the country. Let us not forget that I do not wish to touch upon that point further. Witnesses and parties speaking in Malayalam are examined in the vernacular, and the Judges also understand Malayalam. They sit there and copy them down in the vernacular itself. That is sufficient.

President: Time is up.

A. B. Salem: I, therefore, oppose this resolution, as it will serve no useful purpose to the country.

Debate on February 4, 1926
THE SUPPLY OF ALWAYE WATER TO MATTANCHERI[14]
Alwaye (Aluva) is a town on the banks of the mighty Periyar River and Salem, along with S. S. Koder, was a pioneer in piping water from the river southwards towards Mattancherry and starting a city water supply scheme.

A. B. Salem: That shows how much interest he took in the welfare of the town. That is all that I can say on that point. Sir, whatever be the reason for not doing so in the past, as soon as this House is in possession of the information officially from the Member for Mattancheri, that the people there are suffering for want of drinking water. I say it is the duty of the Government to

---

14 This was how Mattancherry was spelt in documents of the Cochin Kingdom.

do whatever lies in their power to remedy matters.

Now Sir, I don't think it will be possible for us to cut the supply to the Railway, because it is not known whether they use the water for the boilers of for drinking purposes.

S. S. Koder[15]: For boilers, they take from the river.

A. B. Salem: Then, of course, we cannot cut short the supply to the Railway, because it is being supplied to people for drinking purposes at the Railway station.

•••••

S. S. Koder: For loco purposes, for general passengers and so on.

•••••

A. B. Salem: Water is wanted in Mattancherry for the human boilers and the water may be supplied to the Mattancherry Municipality... We also give water (8,00 to 10,00 gallons a day) for the boilers of the Tata Oil Mills... I suppose that this water is also metered.

V. K. Aravindaksha Menon: Yes, the supply to the Tatas is also metered.

A. B. Salem: I don't think any member would say that, because one place is starving for want of drinking water, another place should also be adversely affected. It is our duty to rise to the occasion and find out ways and means for supplying the town of Mattancheri as well with good drinking water. As far as deep boring is concerned, I pretend to speak with some authority on the subject. The Cochin Municipality of which I was a member, before I came over to Ernakulam, had a scheme of well boring.

It was tried in the years 1895 to 1898 in British Cochin for the first time, and the Madras Government, after having spent about Rs. 33,000 upon the well-boring experiment there, and after spending a further sum of money on the recommendation of an Engineer – who recommended the experiment to be continued after an accident had happened, by which the apparatus that was bringing up the sand from the bore fell into the bore itself – abandoned the scheme.

15 Samuel Shabdai Koder (1869–1941) was a Paradesi Jewish Leader and one of the wealthiest merchants in Cochin, who was elected from the general Mattancherry constituency.

He said that, if that is removed, we can get good water, and upon that recommendation, the Madras Government further spent a large sum on money, with the result that at the end of that experiment a sample of the sub-soil of Cochin arranged in a tube, and the earth was sent to the Meteorological Department at Simla.

There they examined sub-soil and pronounced an opinion that there is no good water in such a sub-soil, and the Madras Government also passed a Government order to the effect that good drinking water should not be sought for in Cochin, and that water must be sought for on the mainland, and should, if found, be conveyed across the backwater to British Cochin.

Sir, in the face of that definite order of the Government, the British Cochin Municipality, after some years, went into the question, and, on the recommendation of one Mr. Hutton, wanted a small sum of Rs. 2,000 to be spent for another experiment again. I happened to be a member of the Municipality, and I protested and pointed out that there was a definite Government order that forbade trying any further experiment for water in Cochin.

That was brushed aside with the result that Madras Government spent another sum of Rs. 80,000 or more upon the Cochin well-boring experiment, and was not able to find out water there. They are almost despairing of that while elephant.

I say that is a sufficient warning for us not to spend any money in trying to do the same kind of experiment in Cochin in order to satisfy our desire and laudable ambition to supply water to the inhabitants of Mattancheri.

Sir, there is no other solution for the problem than to convey water – Alwaye water –again into Mattancheri. If we duplicate our plant, in the Waterworks at Chowwara, I think the matter of supplying water to Mattancheri can be solved, and I understand that a scheme for the same is before the Government for consideration.

We should take in view this also, and supply water to Mattancheri. When I was a member of the Mattancheri Municipality and the British Cochin Municipality at one and the same time, I suggested, when the question of the supply of water to Ernakulam town was on the anvil, that, if we were to combine the resources of Mattancheri, British Cochin, and Ernakulam and co-operate with the Darbar for a joint scheme for supplying water to all the three Municipalities, we would be able to materialize the scheme.

But suggestions from money-less people like me are seldom valued, (*Laughter*) and they are repenting for it, and, therefore, Sir, I submit once again that the only possibility of supplying Mattancheri with good water is by conveying water across the back-waters, and this humble request for the supply of 25 to 50 thousand gallons of water is a request that the Government should comply with at the earliest possible moment, even if it be by supplying less water to the inhabitants of Ernakulam.

And I am sure the inhabitants of Ernakulam will only be too glad to stand their water supply being cut short a little for the purpose of supplying drinking water to Mattancheri; and if they would be careful in using their water, I think they can rise to the occasion and cut short the waste of water in Ernakulam.

DEBATE ON THE APPOINTMENT OF A RETRENCHMENT COMMITTEE - 4TH FEBRUARY 1926

President: If the [Retrenchment] Committee is appointed, one thing will be necessary. It will have to inspect officers to understand the strength of the establishments, what the officers are paid, what is the work that will be absolutely necessary and the examination of witnesses also. I do not know how far it is absolutely necessary, I cannot say. You want the report sufficiently earlier, before the next budget session.

...You will have to go and visit the Heads of Departments, go into their offices, see the establishments and the number of clerks, what their duties are, and whether it is possible to do away with some of the clerks, and so on....

A. B. Salem: Sir, I support this resolution. I do not think there will be a single member in this house, either on the official benches or on the non-official benches that will not support this resolution. The practical shape that this resolution should take is the bugbear. What are the terms of reference? How is this grand policy of retrenchment to be carried out? How are we to get effective suggestions for retrenchment?

These are the questions that face us. I have a suggestion, Sir, that instead of having one single Retrenchment Committee, we should have several Retrenchment Committees, so that each of these Committees may be attached to a particular department.

Thus we can simultaneously do intensive work in every department of the Government, as far as the Retrenchment Committee is concerned. We may select three or four men from the non-official members of this House or from outside, and attach them to the Revenue Department with the Diwan Peishkar[16] attached to the Committee.

The Diwan Peishkar would then be able to give all the information with reference to the expenses in the Revenue Department to this Committee. This could be done with men of some experience or with some enthusiasm to study and experiment. They will then be guided in the proper channel and free the difficulties of retrenchment, and they will give us a report on them. If we thus gather the reports in a short time by small committees, we can have a scrutiny carried out in all the various departments soon, and then there is this House as a whole which can consider the reports of these several committees that have gone into the working of the several departments of the state.

If we have one single Committee, Sir, it would be difficult within the short time that will elapse between this and the budget session, to have an elaborate and intensive report of the retrenchment before this House, by the time of the budget session. I very much fear that it would not be possible within that time, even if each of the Departments is scrutinized simultaneously by a Retrenchment Committee.

President: How many Retrenchment Committees do you wish to appoint?

A. B. Salem: I would like to have a Retrenchment Committee appointed in each of the spending departments such as the Public Works Department, Education, Forest etc.

President: We have many spending departments...We will have to appoint many Retrenchment Committees.

16 The *Diwan Peishkar* in the Cochin and Travancore kingdoms exercised powers as the Secretary of State and was in charge of revenue collection and also headed the police and magisterial wings of the administration in their respective districts.

A. B. Salem: Supposing we have got a Scientific Department also besides the Agricultural Department and other minor departments of administration, three or four of these minor departments may be examined by one Retrenchment Committee, and in this way, we will have studied reports, and then we can scrutinize each report, and Government can come to a certain conclusion.

Of course, the difficulty will be in regard to vested interests. I will ask that freshmen or non-officials not contaminated as it were with previous prejudices should be appointed on these committees. For this reason, if we appoint a large number of officials, there will be clash of vested interests with our ideas.

A simple administration should be our aim. We have come to a state in Cochin where the number of people in the jail is very insignificant. I think, out of a population of nearly ten lakhs (one million), the number in the jail is not above 300 a day. That is the state of civilization we have attained.

We have got a very law abiding population in the country, and in such a place it would be the best place to simplify the administration as far as possible and to avoid this present very complicated machinery. We have introduced all these complicated machinery which were suitable for other times, for other conditions elsewhere. We have been plainly copying the Madras administration, where the problems or administration were not identical to the problems in Cochin.

Cochin is more or less a homogeneous area. In spite of all differences of religion – Christian and Nair – all are the same, and if you scratch the skin deep, they will all have the same blood. Ethnographically, we are one unit.

So in these places, Sir, there will be no reason for these communal discriminations and other things. Inside every department, you will find, Sir, there will be no difficulty to cut down expenditure, whoever be the class or people that predominate, and whoever be the members, and whatever caste they come from.

They equally suggest retrenchments, and Sir, in this way, adopt a policy of retrenchment and reduction of hands and simplify the administration. It will be impossible to pay the subordinates handsomely. We are overmanned in the State, and overpaid at the top.

Certainly, Sir, our administration admits of greater simplification, and that would be another way of turning the ideas of the educated people into industrial, commercial and other enterprises by not making Government services very attractive and lucrative, except for the honour of it.

Then we shall find that this hunting after Government employment will also cease in the land to the good of the country. With these few words, I support the resolution, and ask you to consider the question to have Committees rather than one single committee.

DEBATE ON THE MANNER OF ASKING QUESTIONS
FEBRUARY 5, 1926.

A. B. Salem: A point of order. I waited till the last day of this session and till the last hour to raise this point. There are several questions that have been sent up with reference to particular subjects, and the answers have been given piecemeal. It is the ruling of our President that our questions should be fully answered.

Under the circumstances, the question is whether the Government is at liberty to answer questions piecemeal. That is a very important point for us.

We are asking for information for the purpose of elucidating a particular subject with which we are dealing and though we put a certain number of questions - which, though numbered altogether, are published piecemeal with their answers - we will not be in a position to get the exact information. When the questions are split into several parts, and only one or two answers are given every day, we do not get the advantage of calling upon all the answers to the questions.

For instance, with reference to the Anappara Leper Asylum, I had sent in a number of questions, but I find some are still to be answered.

I ask, you Sir, whether it is fair to treat us in this way. Out of the questions sent by us on a particular subject, a few only are answered in this session, and even those that are answered are not answered on one and the same day.

If they are not ready, let them not answer them. I understand from the Secretary to the Diwan that questions on a particular subject have to be answered in most cases by various departments, and the answers do not come in together from the various departments, and the answers that come are entered in the answer papers. That, I submit, need not be done. It is an unsatisfactory procedure.

President: ... I do not understand what you mean by saying that the questions are divided.

A. B. Salem: I will tell you, Sir. Now, I send up 12 questions, numbered 1 to 12, on a particular subject. The Government supplies me with answers, say for 1, 2, 3, 5, 8, and so on. Here you will find that the object of putting the question is not served, because only if I can get the answers for the 12 questions, I can proceed further. I want my questions to be answered in a lot.

•••

On the issue of a leading Mental Hospital in Cochin Kingdom and a 'hospital for those suffering from leprosy'

A. B. Salem: Sir, with reference to Anappara[17], I put a string of questions, and I would have had great satisfaction if these had been answered, and I would have been able to show that a re-examination of the question was necessary. For instance, the objection was about the distance between Anappara and Trichur Town. Trichur got contaminated by having the Asylum in the neighbourhood. I put the question: "Will the Government be pleased to state how far is Anappara from Trichur Town, the distance from Ernakulam to Vendurutti, the distance between Vendurutti and Bolghatti?"[18] These questions were subdivisions. These have not been answered.

•••

A. B. Salem: In the same question, I asked the questions regard-

---

17 Anappara in the northern part of Thrissur Corporation had a famous/notorious mental health centre and was part of popular conversation for decades and later in films: "You will be sent to Anappara." Today, the area is knows as Ramavarmapuram.

18 Venduruthy is a small island off Kochi and part of the greater Willingdon Island. It is approachable only from the Ernakulam backwaters. Bolgatty Island is located off Eranakulam and is also known today as Mulavukadu.

ing the Anappara Leper Asylum[19] and other Asylums of the State.

DEBATE ON COMMUNAL REPRESENTATION 5TH FEB, 1926.

A resolution was introduced by Member K. T. Mathew who said: "It is superfluous to prove to this House that adequate representation has not been given, even as far as possible, to the different communities in the State in Government services."

A. B. Salem: Sir, I rise to second this resolution. It is not, Sir, that we have not excellent principles initiated for the guidance of appointments in the service that we are suffering now, but Sir, it is because these principles and rules that have been laid down have not been adhered to by the bureaucracy in the past. *(Hear, hear).*

I will first of all say the Government of Cochin has laid down excellent rules for the guidance of appointments. Under the rules in the Standing Orders, all classes are eligible.

His Highness's Government does not regard any caste or creed as a ground of civil disability. All classes and castes are alike eligible to hold offices under the Sirkar, provided they have the necessary educational and other qualifications.

• Exception: Appointments of officers in direct charge of the Hindu Religious Institutions under Sirkar management can be held only by caste Hindus;

• Exception 2: Appointments in the Nayar Brigade are exclusively reserved to members of the Nayar community.

• Appointment of Relatives: No Head of Department shall, in exercise of the power vested in him, appoint any relative of his in any office under his control, without the special sanction of the Diwan, nor shall the Diwan appoint any relative of his in the State without the special sanction of His Highness. In regard to all appointments, recommended by Heads of Departments to the Diwan, the recommending officers shall say so clearly, if any of the men recommended happen to be their relatives, and the Diwan shall do the same in regard to all appointments recommended by him to His Highness.

There are only two exceptions to these rules that are provided

---

19 Leprosy is now called Hansen's Disease and is completely curable.

for by the Government. This is in regard to the appointments in Hindu Religious Institutions under Sirkar management and with reference to the Nayar Brigade which are entirely caste-Hindu appointments. Then, Sir, there is an excellent rule, Rule 12 in the same second chapter of the Standing Orders.

These rules have been framed for the purpose of generating satisfaction all around so that no favourites may be appointed in the State, but Sir, what has been the rules in spite of the rules that we have? The greatest number of appointments have gone to caste-Hindus, and all others put together do not come to a third of them.

You see, Sir, from the figures quoted by the Hon'ble Member for Kunnamkulam, that the majority of the appointments are held by the caste Hindus. There are altogether 700 appointments of Government. Non-caste Hindus and all the others put together have not even 200 appointments between them. This shows the way in which the appointments are distributed among the various castes in the State. So I ask the Hon'ble Members on the other side and the President not to recruit any more caste-Hindus. If you had a certain number of appointments given to these non-caste communities, then Government would have been perfectly in order.

This resolution we take as an eye-opener of the session, so that at least in years to come after the Legislative Council has been started there would be satisfaction generated in the matter of the distribution of the loaves and fishes at the disposal of the Government.

Sir, that is the object of this resolution. The inveterate and unresponsive method that has been pursued has brought us to this pass, and therefore, Sir, we hope, although no responsibility directly attaches itself on the Heads of Departments to this house, nevertheless the advice we give the Government, I hope, would be adopted in the spirit in which it is given.

We are aware that none of the Government Officers feel that they are responsible to this House, and that is a fact also. They are not legally responsible to this House today, and in course of time, we shall not fail in our endeavors to make them care more and more for us and to make them feel their responsibilities.

Therefore, in this matter of the distribution of loaves and fishes in the future, all classes of the people should be equally represented in proportion to their numbers and education.

Speaking for the Jews themselves, we have not many grievances, because none of us hold an appointment in any department of the State, and we have had at least a dozen graduates, and it is a pity that our community was driven out through certain causes - whatever they might be, I might not say. For the Government gave us no encouragement.

President: They, do you say that they were driven out?

A. B. Salem: Our educated young men were induced to go away from Cochin elsewhere to seek bread.

President: They are better off for that.

A. B. Salem: They might be materially well off. We have a young Medical graduate who applied for an appointment and he was not given any.

Sir, there is another resolution which stands in my name; otherwise, I would have said a word or two about the selection of the candidates at least to higher Police work. Now Sir, with these words - and we do not wish to express any harsh words - we hope for a better future; we do hope that the Officers of the Government will not recruit caste-Hindus, and would take this in good spirit and make the first endeavour to bring up others in all departments. It is more or less clearly and expressly stated in every part of the country that, wherever a caste-Hindu is placed as the Head of the Department, he tries to bring in caste-Hindus. Whether it is right or wrong, I do not say.

Member Dr. A. R. Menon interjects: Whenever a Christian is appointed as the Head of a Department, he tries to bring in Christian. You never got the opportunity, I say.

A. B. Salem: Both are to be charged. If you had given me an opportunity, I would have shown otherwise. And so, Sir, we hope that in future this resolution would be well-accepted by the Government and we hope the Heads of Departments will act according to the Standing Orders and advise you. You must look to the force of these arguments firstly and see that these grievances are redressed.

•••••

DEBATE ON BILL TO AMEND THE COCHIN COURT OF WARDS REGULATION - NOVEMBER 29, 1926.

A. B. Salem: Sir, I rise to contribute a few words to this discussion, and I waited to see whether the Government would make their position clear in the matter. I never expected, Sir, that the Government of Cochin would bring in a piece of legislation before this House for the sake of giving protection to a particular individual.

It has been abundantly made clear in this House that this piece of legislation has been placed on the anvil for the purpose of giving protection to a particular estate that they have chosen to take under their protection.

President: Generally, it will apply to all the estates, but in this particular case, it will apply immediately.

A. B. Salem: I understand that it is the particular case that has been mentioned in this House that induced the Government to bring this piece of legislation at this juncture before this House. I say that you ought not to have done so, and in a way, Sir, I think it will be a very bad precedent to establish the custom of bringing in a piece of legislation for the purpose of protecting one particular case.

President: This is brought in only to protect the interests of a minor.

A. B. Salem: There is a major in this particular case.

A. B. Salem; Does the Government take up every minor under their protection? I understand the practice in Madras. Suppose he belongs to an old, ancient family of sole status and condition - say - a Zamindar. If the ward is a young gentleman of standing, of an ancient, noble family, if he is involved, and is a minor, then the Government takes him under their protection.

Here is a case where there is no such consideration. If the Government will say what the consideration is and place the information before the House, it will help us to understand the matter. It is only an ordinary case of debt, being an ordinary landlord who is unable to pay off his debts. Is the Government to protect him?

President: All these points have been carefully considered. It is with considerable reluctance that the Government made up its mind to take up the management of this estate.

A. B. Salem: If the information is placed before the House, we will be in a position to say whether it is a fit one, and whether this special emergency Regulation should also be passed.

A BUILDING FOR THE Legislative COUNCIL - 9 DEC. 1925

A. B. Salem: Sir, I rise to oppose the construction of a hall. I perfectly agree with the Hon'ble Member for Public Works (in this regard).

DEBATE ON THE COTTON INDUSTRY (STATISTICAL) BILL

A. B. Salem: I endorse every word of what the Hon'ble members of the opposition said in this House, with reference to this Bill. But I am unable to support the opposition and my loyalty to the British Government and the oath taken by me on the opening day prevent me from opposing this Bill. I do not think the Cochin Government is able to oppose it. That is the situation in which I am placed. *(Hear, hear.)*

I have sworn to His Majesty the King Emperor. His Majesty's Government asks for a particular bill through my Government and my Government brings this Bill, and is not able even to assign a reason for its being passed. This House, no doubt, can express its genuine feelings, and say that this is not done in our interests.

I sympathize with you; and condole with you in the position in which you and I find ourselves as subordinates within the influence of the British power.

But the house will stultify itself, if it goes on considering the opposition; and if it throws out the bill, what will be the result? The Bill will be passed over the head of this House by proclamation. That will be the result. We express our sentiments, and our intellect does not approve of this Bill as necessary to the cotton industry. But we are unable to oppose it, and, therefore, I do not do so.

DEBATE ON THE ESTABLISHMENT OF A STATE BANK
1 DECEMBER, 1926

A. B. Salem: I wanted, Sir, to be a listener to this important resolution than to be a contributor to the discussion. But having heard the very beautiful, eloquent and diplomatic statement of the Revenue Member, I rise to congratulate him as the best charming player on the harp of the Government. Shall I characterize his statement as the best piece of official hypocrisy, and if that be a strong word, I would say his was a diplomatic way of putting things.

Sir, I am not here to support the statements that have fallen from the Members regarding Cochinites as 'Invertebrates' with a capital "I". I emphatically protest against it. I say, Sir, there are many vertebrates here. If the Cochin people are invertebrates, then the Government which draws its men from them are equally invertebrates. I do not subscribe to it.

K. S. Rama Ayyar: I never said, Sir, that the people of Cochin are invertebrates. I never meant any reflection.

•••••

A. B. Salem: Then, I shall come to the business. The Cochin Government has been here before the Trichur Bank. Now, the Trichur Bank is a bank composed of Cochinites. In answer to question 70 of the budget session of 1100, an answer was elicited from the Government to show that Indian Bank which came here only the other day had two and quarter lakhs deposited by the Cochin Government there, and Nedungadi Bank Rs. 80,000, and the Imperial Bank Rs. one lakh and ten thousand.

The National Bank had Rs. 3 lakhs and 15 thousand, and what did the Cochin people's Bank have? The Trichur Bank is a Cochin people's Bank. It had only Rs. 50,000.

Now, I ask you, is that patronizing a local bank? Is that the sympathy that has been boasted by the Revenue Member? Is that practical sympathy or is that the only big sympathy? That is the question I put.

We have had several bitter experiences, and therefore, I say this. Trust begets trust. If you trust a man, he will trust you in return; Like begets like all over the world; and I cannot imagine a greater sin on the part of the Government that not to trust its own people.

The Government must trust its people and the people must trust the Government. That is the most happy state of affairs, and if the people and the Government trust one another, there is no reason why banks should not spring up here, manned by local men and local capital to do the little work we have here.

I say, Sir, that co-operation has not been called for - has not been drawn out in the country, and that is the reason why we are economically depressed. There is much talent, but encouragement has not been sufficient.

Let me ask, Sir, one question. "Is there one country in the world that can call herself progressive that has not waded through seas of failures?" The South Sea Bubble, the Arbuthnot failure, these are all colossal failures that the people have gone through. Similarly, there was the Alliance Bank failure.

Failures are stepping stones to success. Supposing the tanneries fail, the potteries fail, is that sufficient reason to say, "You have failed once; you will not succeed any more?" I have been advocating here that the Government has no commercial brain or commercial talent. They must stand apart and encourage.

Rao Sahib T. V. Kasturi Ranga Ayyar: You come with a bank. We will render all possible help.

A. B. Salem: I am very glad to hear that statement. You will see that, within 7 days, a bank will come to you. I hope you will fulfill your sympathy in a practical manner ... Within seven days, I shall form a committee.

•••••

A. B. Salem: May I know the state of investment today, Sir, in the foreign banks?

President: We have not got figures now.

A. B. Salem: We only want to know roughly; that is all. How much has been invested in the Indian Bank, the National Bank and the Imperial Banks? May I know the investment in any of the Cochin local banks?

President: We have invested some amount in the Imperial Bank and some in the Indian National Bank also.

K. Krishna Pisharodi: Nothing in the Indian Bank.

A. B. Salem: May I know whether there is any money of the Cochin Government lying in any of the banks registered in the Cochin State and doing work here in Cochin territory? May I know whether one single rupee is remaining in any of the Cochin banks today? Why don't you answer "yes" or "no"?

Rao Sahib T. V. Kasturi Ranga Ayyar: Is the Member in order?

A. B. Salem: The information is with you Sir, your books will show.

President: You should not address Members personally.

A. B. Salem: I addressed through you, Sir.

President: You should not violate the rules of decorum of the Council in discussion. We will now rise.

The House rose for the day at 5:00pm.

Recorded by T. K. Krishna Menon, Secretary to the Council

DEBATE CONTINUES ON THE ESTABLISHMENT OF A STATE BANK 2 DECEMBER, 1926

A. B. Salem: The Trichur Bank is not the only bank that has applied to our Government for deposit. I am informed that several banks having a large reserve fund like the Chittur Bank have also applied to the Government asking for deposits, which the Government has refused.

I can very well understand the reason why the Government denied to disclose the real facts concerning the refusal. That may be a reflection upon the bank. Whose business credit in the market is likely to be shaken? There may be also so many other reasons.

So I do not want to ask such questions. Let me try to make you understand that the reasons for a private bank in Cochin in approaching for a Government deposit would be for inspiring the confidence for the people to deposit their money there.

This would be a sort of encouragement for the private banks. If the people, by some devices, get the information that a private bank applied to the Government for deposit, and the Government declined, surely it will affect the credit of the bank.

On the other hand, if a deposit is given by the Government, the bank will get a standing in the place, and inspire the confidence of the country. That is the aspect of the question. The advantages of a bank are innumerable. The encouragement to trade is one of the many facilities afforded by banks in a country.

After all, the Government may lose a few rupees. I can say that the primary consideration of the Government in investing deposits is the safety of the funds invested. It is also incumbent on the Government to encourage their subjects in this business.

Even if the Government would lose a few rupees, I say the risk is worth having. I hope the Government will consider this aspect of the question also, whenever applications are sent to them.

•••••

President: The Government is just like any other private body as regards the investment of money. They will consider its stability and soundness of its management and if they are satisfied, they will probably deposit money in it.

A. B. Salem: Cannot the Government impose certain conditions, when an application comes - that a bank should be so and so and that upon these conditions, it can lend money? Why should we be running in a circle and say how can we be expected to inspire confidence in you, before you have confidence in us? That will be running in a circle.

President: Why should you go and ask for loans from the Government? Without loans, you can carry on your business.

A. B. Salem: That is possible only in self-governing countries. Let us take the case of the Bank of England. It is in a country which governs itself. It is the people's bank. People govern it. It lends money to the Government. Whenever the Government wants money, they go to the bank and ask them "Will you raise a loan from America or anywhere else?"

Here that is not the case. We have to look to the Government for encouragement for everything. There you have hundreds of hospitals - Bartholomew Hospital, this hospital, that hospital and a number of other hospitals can be quoted. But here in this country all the good hospitals are Government hospitals. Here everything is the other way. That is the difficulty. If it is a people's Government, and if a particular minister from a particular party has a bank in its power, he will say that the Government should help that bank as much as possible. In this way the country prospers. But here that is not the case. Here we have a stable, fixed, irremovable Government, and we cannot influence it. It can only influence us. These are the facts to be considered.

DEBATE ON MOTION UNDER STANDING ORDER 19 (1)
3RD DECEMBER, 1926

A. B. Salem: I think it is a substantive right. Kindly refer to S. O. 19 (2). There it is said: "Save as otherwise provided for in the Rules or Standing Orders, a Member who wishes to move a motion shall give notice of his intention to the Secretary 6 clear days before the meeting at which he intends to move the motion, provided that the President may, in his discretion, admit at any time any motion at shorter notice than that prescribed by any order or may admit a motion without notice."

We have got several things such as motion, resolution, etc. A motion is defined in Standing Order 2. A motion means a proposal made by a Member for the consideration of the Council relating to any matter which may be discussed by the Council, and includes an amendment.

A resolution means a motion for the purpose of discussing matters of general public interest. So any proposal made by a Member for the consideration of the Council becomes a motion in itself. How can those motions be moved?

A resolution requires 15 days' notice, a question 12 days', and a motion 6 days'. This may be modified according to the discretion of the President. There is a substantive right of the Members to make a motion. A motion is a substantive move for bringing in a resolution.

The rights conferred by a motion and a resolution are different substantive rights. In the case of motions the Government must be given 15 day's clear notice, and in the other case, of resolutions 6 day's, which may or may not be insisted upon, according to the discretion of the President. So I submit that the motion under S.O. 19 (2) is a substantive right of the Council.

.....

Salem argues on many points with members of the house.

A. B. Salem: The object of the Regulation is to discuss any matter of importance. The function of the Council is that.

......

A. B. Salem: Section 11. It says the matters that are mentioned in section 11 are excluded from the consideration or enactment of the Council. So every matter that does not come within the walls of that section and which is of importance to the public can be discussed here.

......

A. B. Salem: The right as to what all matters can be discussed here is not stated there. What all matters cannot be discussed are given. If these things do not find a place in these Rules, they can be discussed by means of motions, resolutions, Bills etc.

......

A. B. Salem: Then, how was it moved, if it was not provided for in the Rules?

......

A. B. Salem: Where is it stated that an official Member can move a resolution without it going to the ballot box? They have not the right to move any resolutions; They have only to defend their action.

......

A. B. Salem: Official members have no right to move a resolution. I shall show the force of my argument. Here the House consists of elected representatives, nominated people, Government officials and the Diwan. We discuss matters. You have been good enough to say that each officer has certain functions delegated to him. Now, the resolution is a recommendation made to the Government. Can the Government recommend anything to themselves? Can I recommend anything to myself, if I want a certain thing to be done? If the Government wants to do a certain thing, they can do it for themselves.

......

A. B. Salem: Any matter which requires the decision of the Council may at once be brought here by a motion, if you want to have the sense of the Council.

•••••

A. B. Salem: I do not know where it is so stated. Where is the rule that says that the resolutions brought forward by the Government Members need not go to the ballot box? It was never contemplated that the official members should bring in resolutions. It is not the Government but the Council that recommends.

DEBATE ON A BUILDING FOR THE LEGISLATIVE COUNCIL

A. B. Salem: Sir, I rise to oppose the construction of a hall. I perfectly agree with the Hon'ble Member for the Public Works Department in saying that these are hard times of poverty when the Government should exercise great caution.

My great regret, however, is that after a large sum of money was spent for the construction of a Leper Asylum[20] already built; there is going to be another.

I think, after having heard what fell from the lips of the Hon'ble Member for Public Works, the Chief Engineer, the Government will not hesitate to reconsider the scheme on which they have to spend much of public money.

When the consideration of spending the money comes before them, I hope they will consider the weighty observations of the Chief Engineer regarding these hard times, etc., and it is the same consideration that make me rise to oppose this resolution.

The questions of constructing a new Legislative Council building my be considered when "better times turn up", to use the words of the ex-Secretary to the Government. That is the reason why I oppose the resolution. Otherwise, I would certainly have supported the resolution.

I came to the hall with the intention of supporting the resolution. But after having had the advantage of hearing the Chief Engineer, I have changed my opinion (*Laughter*) upon the question of economy; and therefore, I hope the mover will also change his opinion. The Government also changed their opinion with regard to the Anappara Leper Asylum. With these few words, I rise to op-

---

20 Palliport Leper Asylum, about 25 km from Ernakulam, bequeathed by the Dutch.

pose the resolution for the construction of a new hall anywhere in the whole State.

•••••

VOTING FOR DEMANDS FOR SUPPLEMENTARY GRANTS - 23RD FEBRUARY, 1927

Supplementary Grant of Rs. 1,000 under General Administration - Huzur Secretariat - Special Finance Committee

A. B. Salem: We do not want to see Government servants leaving their legitimate duties and sitting in the House. I request the Government to take early steps to introduce responsible government, and fill those seats with Ministers, Secretaries and Parliamentary Secretaries, who will do their duty properly and with pleasure.

President: Till then, you are not going to allow this demand *(Laughter).*

A. B. Salem: I ask you to consider these things. Making these Supplementary Demands is giving the Members an opportunity to criticize the administration. If no Demands are made, we get no chance.

With these few remarks, I should fervently hope that the House would grant them, This demand is a particular matter for the Special Finance Committee which the Government has created and which is doing work in different directions. I do not press this motion to a division.

President: Please keep your speeches to the point at issue.

T. K. Krishna Menon: After having had his say in his most eloquent way, criticizing with all force the administration, he quietly withdraws his motion. I think he is afraid of getting a smart answer from the Government Members.

A. B. Salem: Sir, I do not withdraw. The officials may have their say.

The Motion was put to vote and carried.

•••••

Motion No. 4. - *To reduce the allotment of Rs. 7,652 under "IX - Forests Act" by one rupee.*

A. B. Salem: Sir, I have tabled this token motion to call attention to the fact that a large quantity of rosewood[21] has been under contract to be supplied from the forests of Cochin to a particular contractor. I am not concerned with names and I do not want to enter into the merits of any particular contractor. But this contract is standing in the way of people inside Cochin State getting rosewood from our forests.

There are many people who are willing and anxious to get rosewood till this contract is over. This particular contract, I understand, has got still a large balance to be supplied to fulfil it, and Cochinites, who are coming forward for rosewood, cannot get rosewood from the forests.

It is stated, till this contract is fulfilled, no rosewood could be got. That seems to me a very great hardship. If there is sufficient and more in the forests to fulfill that contract, I do not see why the extra quantity that is available cannot be supplied to applicants who want rosewood.

ADJOURNMENT MOTION FOR PURPOSES OF DEBATE

(Salem, who was fighting his own private battles over religious rights in the Paradesi Synagogue, was vociferous about the rights of various Hindu social groups who were barred by the so-called upper castes from entering temples on the grounds that were not 'pure' enough. In this debate, Salem attacks the concept of inequality and untouchability "the cancerous growths of Hinduism.")

A path used by parishioners of the Njarrakal Church[22] to carry corpses was ordered closed by local authorities, The District Magistrate advised that the road be closed, and the order was seen to benefit the powerful Paliam family[23]. It was also charged by Mem-

---

21 Rosewood is a richly-coloured timber, brown with dark veins and grows wild in the forests of the Sahyadri Mountains of Kerala. *Dalbergia sissoo,* as it is known to science, is dense, strong, aromatic and comparable to teakwood. Trees have been dated in the Ayyappankoil ranges to 700 years and in the Nenmara and Neliympatty forests to around 500 years.

22 The Njarakkal Church was established in 1451 and continued to be an active congregation of the Archeparchy of Ernakulam-Angamaly.

23 Members of the Paliam Family were traditional Prime Ministers of the Cochin Kingdom.

ber C. A. Ouseph that the path obstructed the movement of Ezhava children who used it to go to school.

C. A. Ouseph: The Government has openly sided with the Paliam and advised them to put gates on the road. By obstructing, they have negatived the rights of the depressed classes. The Christians too would be prevented from passing through that road and taking corpses. To put up a gate would be placing some restraint on free passage ... violating all rules of natural justice. I support the motion [to undo the order].

A. B. Salem: I raise to support the motion. There is no heat in me with reference to this motion. I looked at it with complete detachment. I find from the map here (*holding the map in hand*) Sir, that this road is the continuation of a road. A single road passes through the entire map and goes from this end and goes on, I do not know how far.

Therefore, this road which is now supposed to be closed is only part of an old road, and certainly it cannot be supposed that the people of Nayarambalam – be they Ezhavas, or Christians, or Jews or Mohamadans could not have been passing through that road. There is sufficient evidence before this House to the fact that these roads have been used by the public at large.

There is a decision of the court. I shall tell you; the evidence is that the District Magistrate, in 1099, when a dispute arose decided in favour of the Christians passing through this road. And I know of no road through which a Christian passes which is closed to the Ezhavas in Cochin!

I do not know. It has been stated here in reply to question that in the whole of the Cochin state there is only half a mile of road that is closed to Ezhavas, that is in Thrippunithura and Irinjalakkuda. All other roads are open to all castes, That was the statement made by the Government.

A. B. Salem: I think the question was not asked of metalled roads along. You find here this road which passes by the supposed temple site is also a continuation of another road of very great length going to the *thodu* (*thodu is an irrigation canal*) from somewhere south – far south.

Therefore, there is absolutely no justification of any kind for us here to hold a view that it was at any time closed to Ezhavas. I, therefore, say that the Government has erred and seriously erred in these times of removal of untouchability when the whole of India, is going to nationalize itself to fight against a higher and cleverer civilization of exploitation, when they are going to unite into a single compact nation of importance by the removal of untouchability in giving their services to the higher instead of to the lower people.

When the different sections are trying to weld themselves into one, what do we find here? We find the Government of Cochin is not moving with the times. It pains me hard and it is a great grievance to me as a citizen of Cochin to tell the Government that it is not apparently aware of this unification of the whole population of the whole land.

I am sure, Sir, that there will not be a patriotic soul in the whole length and breadth of Cochin to say that we should not take our part in this great unification (*Hear, hear*) that is going to come.

We cannot, therefore, leave back a section of the population, almost twenty seven percent, and we must carry them along with us. We must stretch every point to give them that right and to make them feel that they are one with us, and that they are part and parcel of the great polity of Cochin. And the nationalization of this land will not also take place unless the higher castes come forward and say to the lower: "YOU BROTHERS, we must get you up and take you along the road of progress."

I am extremely pleased to hear the Hon'ble Member of Irinjalakkuda who had supported this proposition in most eloquent terms. He being a high caste Hindu, it cannot but have a very desirable effect upon the higher castes in Cochin.

I therefore, think Sir, that this is a proposition in which every Member of this House would stand up and say in clear words that the action of the authorities with reference to their right to obstruct the passage to the lower castes should be countenanced by this House or by the Government with disfavour.

Our advice to the Government would be to direct the District Magistrate to give instruction to the policemen to uphold the right of all human beings to pass through that road, and not to come to a compromise over it at all.

Compromise is not a remedy for evil and it will certainly bring down on the body politic undesirable effects. Non-cooperate with evil and not with good. Now, what is the remedy suggested? The construction of a new road. That means some more pressure on the tax-payers, and this is no remedy. That is merely a make-shift.

Now, what is pollution? One can understand it as a flutter from delusion. In this instance, the opposite party is the premier land-lord of the Cochin State whose ancestors were the hereditary Prime Ministers of this State.

Certainly, he would give land for a new road. Now, in the case of this particular temple, if they find that it is close to the road, they could take temple far away from the road, so that private rights and private privileges may be exercised without any hindrance whatever from the polluting feet of the Ezhavas.

Certainly this is the policy to be adopted and we want it to be impressed upon the Government. Now, I have got absolutely no intention to wound the feelings of anybody.

There may be honest people among the high caste Hindus and I would suggest every friend of Ezhava reform to consider such honest claims of the high caste Hindus, and they must also give up fighting for their rights so that they may get the sympathy of other classes all over.

Now, ignorance stands in their way. If they find honest men educated enough and able to know what is right and what is wrong, and who should know that this distinction should be washed away into the Indian Ocean before India can unite itself, asking them to get out of the way they should with all manliness stand upon the spot and take the consequences whatever they may be.

I would also at the same time request my Ezhava friends to respect every old woman who passes by on the road, and remove himself to allow her to pass on, so that her feelings may not be wounded. To the social reformers, I would venture to suggest at the same time a manly venture in this direction.

I would tell them, Sir, that if the Government sends two police-men to block this road they are to go and stand there. In Vaikom what was the result? It attracted all India's attention. All went to

Vaikom to maintain the liberal policy in Travancore.[24]

People from far out Punjab – Akalis[25] opened a kitchen at Vaikom. For what purpose? They did not know anything about our customs, manners etc, they could not taste our food, they were like fishes out of water. The whole thing was done for the one feeling of unification and they went there and spent money, spent their energy and worked for the people.

With what motive? To take away from Hinduism its cancerous growths. That was the object and what was the result? Travancore, which stood by the side of the caste Hindus, welcomed Mahatma Gandhi into their Royal House and Her Highness, the Maharani Regent Of Travancore, said "I shall be very pleased to pass orders with the weight of all authority so that My Government shall give all help to the uplift of the poorer classes, and We shall not be a party to maintain these cancerous growths of My Religion."

And what do we find here today? Our Cochin Government which always tell us from the chair we are following Travancore in all important matters – is telling us "Please don't make any disturbance; we will effect a compromise and we will give you another road." Here Cochin is not following Travancore. I should say Cochin should go ahead of Travancore. I would be very pleased if a band of right thinking high caste men would take some Ezhavas all over the place and show that they should all be treated as one.

•••••

CUSTOMS REVENUE

A. B. Salem: One of the sources of federal revenue is the customs - true, we have provided safeguards but nobody is going to change the constitution for us. We will be deprived of our customs.

---

24 The Vaikom Satyagraha (1924–25) was a protest movement in the then Travancore Kingdom against untouchability in Hindu society. The protest was centered around the Sri Mahadeva Temple at Vaikom and it soon snowballed into a national movement with Mahatma Gandhi and others stepping in to allow all sections of the people entry into the temple.

25 Akalis were members of the Sikh temple reform movement which was launched in the 1920s. ('Akal' means 'immortal'. The Akalis participated in the protest at the Vaikom Shiva temple.)

The Federal Committee have foreseen this and hence their demand for the amount we had expended in the Harbour also. If such a state should come to pass, have we not lost all the benefits you have secured for us at great exertion and with consummate tact in the settlement of the Harbour question?

Nobody had hitherto given expression to the advantages by joining the Federation. We, poor folk, excluding, of course, the nine knowing gentlemen of the Federal Committee require some tuition in the matter. Our kith and kin of British India will be against us in the matter.

One great personage of international fame, in response to my request to champion our cause, said that it would be against his interest. After due consideration of the pros and cons one is driven to exclaim why join the federation and be content to play second fiddle to the people outside the State. There is a ray of hope that the contingency will not arise in the near future.

The committee wants to retain all the jurisdiction the Sirkar now has over the Harbour. The pro-federationists go a step further and say that federation necessarily involved a sacrifice or a surrender of certain elements of Sovereignty on the part of the States.

Your reference in your speech day before yesterday of this gives a little consolation to some of us who have only inadequate knowledge of the problem. But I cannot for a moment think that you are treading on sure ground when you say that the entry of Indian States into the scheme of Federation will not act as a drag on the political progress of India.

Can the advance party - the Congress party which is prepared for full independence including cessation from England expect any help from the representatives of the Princes in the Federal Assembly? Have not the Princes been playing hitherto the tune of Imperialistic Britain? We find no change for the better in them. Such being the case, the fear expressed in certain quarters is neither unreasonable nor unfounded.

Unless and until the States have a constitution allied to that in British India, have a responsible Government and the people send their representatives to the Federation, these States will be a drag on the progress of India towards full independence. What if the stipulations, reservations, safeguards which are included in the final memorandum shared the fate of the historical 'scrap of paper'? We abide with forlorn hope.

Sir, I request you kindly convey the loyal greetings and elicitations of my constituents and myself to His Highness our beloved Maharaja.

•••••

INTRODUCTION OF HAND-SPINNING IN SCHOOLS
- December 10, 1925

(The spinning wheel or the 'charkha', for making thread from cotton and other fibres, is believed to have come to India from Persia in the 13th century. Indian independence leader, Mahatma Gandhi, began projecting it in the 1920s as an instrument to promote self-sufficiency and self-rule. In later years, it led to the call to boycott textiles imported from England. The 'charkha' was also the emblem on the flag used by the Congress Party during the independence movement.).

C. Mathai: ...There are people ready to buy these things [the *khadi* or rough cotton cloth made by the *charkha*]. and this gives an added zest to the children. We do not give any grants and I think that is perhaps an argument in favour of the thing... We have not got much of spare funds. I shall briefly sum up the attitude of the Government. We adopt an attitude of sympathy. We appreciate the utility of the thing. We would like the thing extended as much as possible... and we will see how the thing progresses.

A. B. Salem: My amendment is to make it easy for the Government to accept this resolution as a compulsory handicraft in all schools.

My amendment is - Between the words "handicraft" and "made a compulsory" add optional and delete "compulsory."

Then the resolution will read thus - "That this Council recommends to the Government that, in order that hand-spinning be revived as a supplementary industry among the people of the state, the Department of Education may be directed to take necessary steps to introduce hand-spinning as an optional handicraft in all the schools of the State."

Dr. A. G. Menon: It is not an amendment. The chief point is compulsion and the world "optional" changes the whole meaning of the resolution. It is negatived. I have my own doubt whether it is not negativing the proposition. It is not an amendment.

A. B. Salem: I understand the Hon'ble mover's object is to introduce spinning as a handicraft in all the schools of the state as a compulsory subject. If it is made optional, students may join. Five members of each class may like to join the spinning class. In some class, none may like to join.

But if you make it compulsory, it would mean that every student will have to go through the spinning class; and if you do not make it optional in any particular school, there may be parents who object to the spinning craft and ask them not to go to that school. Any student in any class may go there for half an hour a day. My object was to frustrate this and make it optional till we reach such advancement in time as would permit compulsion.

Since that is not possible, I would like to have it introduced as an optional subject. When that advancement comes, we shall make it compulsory. Till then, we have to run the class in every institution on an optional basis. I do not think I was understood properly, when I was objected to.

•••••

DEBATE ON BILL TO AMEND THE COCHIN ABKARI REGULATION- NOVEMBER 28, 1927

The bill was moved by K. Achyuta Menon - Regulation 1 of 1077.

K. Achyuta Menon: The amendment proposed is with regard to the search of houses, which could not now be done by aminadars[26] without a warrant.

(The proposal here was to give more powers to the aminadars to detect the illicit manufacture of liquor. There was always a delay in getting search warrants from magistrates and that aminadars, being senior officials, should be invested with more powers. The status of the Aminadar in

---

26 *Aminadars* were excise officials, equivalent in status to Head Constables in a police station and responsible for collection of taxes related to items like alcohol and tobacco.

Cochin was equivalent to that of Police Station Officer with a salary of between Rs. 15 to Rs. 40. In British India, police station officers could execute searches for illicit liquor and in the neighbouring Kingdom of Travancore, the Aminadars had already been given such powers.)

K. Achyuta Menon: The amendment proposed is nothing extraordinary.

A. B. Salem: May we know the present difficulty experienced with reference to the administration of the department, that is with reference to the searches that is now being experienced because of the absence of power to search to the *aminadars?*

K. Achyuta Menon: The *aminadars* used to search and take possession of liquor when it is found in the premises and *verandahs* of houses. There was a case like that, and when it came to the Chief Court it held that the *aminadars* could not search the *verandah* because it formed part of the house ... Getting a warrant from the magistrate....[takes time] ... and it will be easy for the persons concerned to remove all traces of such an offence.

A. B. Salem: I rise to oppose and to state that our party is also opposed to it. We feel that this power of search can never be vested in the Excise Department. After a great deal of agitation in the time of Mr. Banerji we succeeded in separating the judicial and executive functions of this state.

Rao Sahib T. V. Kasturi Ranga Ayyar: There was no agitation and the separation was no result of agitation.

A. B. Salem: Say it was made as result of co-agitation then. Whatever it is, the matter was well being agitated in the press at the time everywhere, that the judicial and executive functions should be separated, and that it is detrimental to the peace of the State or any State outside in India. If it was done without anyone having pressed for it, then give the credit to Mr. Banerji for having brought about that reformation in Cochin.

It is still our pride that we have advanced far ahead of British India, and as our Member for Thrippunithura has stated the judicial and executive functions have been standing separated here.

President: I think there also the Tehsildars have no magisterial powers.

Rao Sahib T. V. Kasturi Ranga Ayyar: There the Tehsildars (revenue officers) have magisterial powers. They do not exercise them. There, the power is potential.

A. B. Salem: Our *Peishkar* (the main civil administrator) and Tehsildars have been carrying on their revenue collection without magisterial powers, and we have been satisfied with the persuasive element in the administration.

The Excise Superintendents also have been carrying on this department without this power all these years. I do not see why the present Excise Superintendent must cry for Travancore methods now for issuing warrants for the purpose of searching for illicit manufacture of liquor, etc.

What they are asking for now is that they should be given powers to open the doors of people at midnight to search for illicit liquor. Government is openly selling liquor. Government is maintaining a distillery to feed the population with their liquor and increase their liquor appetite.

Government is doing that which they say other people should not do. That is the system under which we are now living. I should have stated that, when the Government tells the people not to do a certain thing and not to manufacture drink, they should set an example by not contributing their own manufacture of liquor, which they are not doing. And they tell you that you must not manufacture liquor.

That is the position in Cochin; it is the same in India. That which you tell others not to do, you ought not to do yourself. Then, under these circumstances when we are crying for as little power to be given to the executive, we are finding an encroachment of the subjects' rights being brought in to be passed here. We are to be searched by the Police, by the Magistrate, by Police Inspectors, by Sub-Inspectors, by the Station House Officers, and now you want to allow the low-paid *aminadars* also come in to search.

I asked a question of the Hon'ble Law Member to enlighten us upon the necessity of this legislation, and I do not get any enlightenment in reply. I get a case, taken before the Chief Court, of an *aminadar* searching the verandah of a house and the Chief Court has said that it was not right.

What is the inference to be drawn from that statement? Even now, when they got no powers, they encroach upon the rights of the people. They get into the houses and abuse their present powers. Who knows how many such cases occur and do not come into public view?

I think, Sir, that it will be detrimental to the public interests to invest these officers with these powers, and we must stoutly oppose the placing of any judicial power in the hands of the Superintendent or the *aminadars* or of any officer of the Department.

Judicial functions should be separate from the executive functions. What is stated here is that there will be liquor in a room, and by the time an Excise Officer goes to the Magistrate for a search warrant, the liquor will go off.

How did he know that there will liquor there? If he has got some information, let him go to the Magistrate first. Why should he look into the house and ascertain whether there is liquor there before he goes to the Magistrate and take the warrant and come into the house for making a search? Now, what is it that he wants? Why do they want to enter our houses?

V. B. Vaidyanath Ayyar: This is not the law.

A. B. Salem: What is the law? We do not want these powers to be given to *aminadars* and Excise peons. They are themselves to be abolished in the near future. We do not want to give them power and then abolish them. Further, our leader's question as to what the proposals of the Special Finance Committee are on the matter has not been answered, In the face of the proposals of the Finance Committee, I do not know whether this Bill itself will be necessary. I oppose the Bill.

•••••

DEBATE ON THE DRESS OF OFFICERS, VAKILS ETC.
December 12, 1927.

Some council members said they supported the kind of dress generally used in the country (and it is not a European dress) by officers, *vakils* (lawyers) and gentlemen.

K. S. Rama Ayyar: People here generally do not use boots and trousers and these things. They do not generally ape the Europeans as some do.

President: He [the official] must be allowed to use what he likes best and should not ape it. Where is the rule laid down for the dress?

•••••

At this point. S. S. Koder, who was also a Jewish representative on the council, also opposed the motion.

S. S. Koder: ...Has the Cochin Legislative Council come to this position towards the end of its first tier that it has to deliberate, discuss and take part in a discussions as to what sort of dress should be worn by an officer, vakil, school-master, clerk and a menial servant when he attends offices, court and school... Have we got nothing else to discuss or deliberate except this question of second cloth or first cloth?

... It would have been very interesting to hear what sort of jacket or jumper a lady should wear when she attends such offices, as I am sure, we have lady doctors, lady teachers, and I do not know if we have lady typists in the services, whether they should be full-sleeved or half-sleeved or sleeveless... I wonder if the mover has left out this important item.

S. F. Nunez: ... Officials are compelled on ceremonious occasions to put on black woollen clothes, especially when attending banquets, just like the lawyers' black dress.

A. B. Salem: The colour must be black. They have limitations also and not necessarily woollen patterns. There are many people who wear *khadi*.

President: It is only in turban and long cloth that there is compulsion, if at all.

•••••

On the death of Sir Diwan Bahadur Perungavur Rajagopalachari, K.C.S. I., C.I.E., MA & BL.[27] - DECEMBER 12, 1927

A. B. Salem: On behalf of the Jewish constituency which I have

---

27 Diwan Bahadur P. Rajagopalachari, (March 18 1862–December 1, 1927) was the Diwan (chief minister) of Cochin State from December 1896 to August 1901 and of Travancore from 1906 to 1914. An able administrator, he was instrumental in setting up bodies that evolved into the Indian Chamber of Commerce and Industry (Cochin) and the Kerala State Archives Department. In 1920, he was elected as the first president of the Madras Legislative Council.

the honour to represent here, I wish to first associate myself with the deep sense of sorrow and grief at the death of Sir P. Rajagopalachari, and to say a few personal words.

I owe my entire career to the great soul of P. Rajagopalachari. Twenty-seven years ago, I approached him as a forlorn boy just come out of the Ernakulam College on his way to Madras, and stopped at Krishna Vilas, at the Easwara-Seva-Madham as it was then called, and met Sir P. Rajagopalachari, Diwan of Cochin, as the Jewish student.

Sir, the great administrator and statesman that he was, he did not stand on red-tapism when heart-felt matters were brought to him. I told him, 'Sir, I stand in need of education, I have no money to study,' and the great soul, in three hours' time, was able to get the Diwan Peishkar to issue a memorandum, which I preserve as a heirloom to be handed down to posterity, of giving me the grant of a liberal scholarship to pursue my study in the Presidency College at Madras.

My heart is full of gratitude to him. I have always cherished his name while he was alive, and I owe him many acts of kindness, everything, at his hands, and I wish to only add that his great ideas with which he guided the Legislative Council of Madras will permeate here, and those great ideas of his will move us also in the march of progress in Cochin. With these few words, I also pay my humble tribute to the great soul.

•••••

Salem was close to the noted Ezhava community leader, social activist and rationalist Sahodaran Ayyappan[28] (1889-1968), whose revolutionary message to the people was 'No Caste, No Religion, No God for Man.' Ayyappan successfully contested the election to the Cochin Legislative Council in 1928, retaining the seat for the next 21 years.

Salem and Ayyappan had the same approach to social problems and supported each other in the Council on many issues. In 1930, when Ayyappan introduced the Cochin Thiyya Bill - to remove the

---

28 Ayyappan was given the title of Rao Sahib by the British Emperor in 1943. In 1935, the Maharaja of Cochin presented him with a 'Veera Shringala' (a golden chain of honour) for his community work. The *Ezhavas* form the largest segment of Kerala HIndus.

matrilineal system of inheritance among the Thiyya[29] community in the Cochin-Ernakulam area, Salem was one of the members of a Select Committee appointed to prepare a report. No amendments were made to the bill - which also penalized bigamy and allowed for inter-marriages between classes and castes. The bill was passed on July 29, 1932.

•••••

A B. Salem's second stint in the Cochin Legislative Council from 1939 to 1945 did not see many fiery speeches - except one on hoarding of food during the war years. He had mellowed considerably by then and much of his battles in the Paradesi Synagogue had ended. He was also conscious of the realities of political life in Cochin that was soon to be radicalized in unexpected ways.

The Indian Independence Movement was gathering pace and communist ideology was taking root in the rural areas of Malabar, Cochin and Travancore. Also, younger leaders had emerged in the labour unions and in small towns and villages, supplanting the moderation espoused by Salem and others who followed the Gandhian ways of non-violent protest.

On one occasion, however, he blasted the idea of India suffering under British rule. When discussing an unrelated matter, Salem went on a tangent to fulminate against imperialist control... "Is the British Government going to go bag and baggage from India? ...What is it that has happened during the last 150 years in India? We have been emasculated completely..."

•••••

BUDGET·SESSION 1116 - August 1, 1941

The Council met in the Council Hall, Ernakulam, with the Hon'ble President Achyuta Menon Avl., B.A., B.L., in the Chair

ELECTIONS TO THE CHALAKUDI PANCHAYAT

Dr. A. R. Menon (Minister for Rural Development): There is

---

29 The *Thiyyas* are clubbed along with the *Ezhava* community as Other Backwards Classes in Kerala today. There is a movement, however, by the *Thiyyas* of Malabar to claim a distinct identity of their own and demand a separate reservation quota in various sectors. They also claim to have originally come to Kerala from regions around the Aegean Sea, while the *Ezhavas* are believed to have arrived from Sri Lanka.

a section of the community called *Viswakarmas*.[30] They are hold-ing meetings and passing resolutions that they are not properly represented. It so happened that I was able to get an educated and qualified man of that sect from this place. He belongs to the *That-tan* (goldsmith) community, and I nominated him. It is very dif-ficult to give representation to all the sub-sections, but as far as possible the principle is followed.

A. B. Salem: May I know whether an Ezhava candidate stood for election (for they have a population of 1,000) in the Panchayat (village administration)?

A. B. Salem: May I know whether there are Nayars (Nairs) in this Panchayat?

•••••

Salem was one of the few legislators who had a sweeping vi-sion about the importance of education in the life of a society and inhabitants.

He became a pioneer in the spread of universal education in Kerala - and the result was there for all to see in the decades that followed, propelling the state of Kerala to become free India's first state to achieve full literacy.

He was among the first to articulate this vision with a call to the Cochin government on August 11, 1941, when he introduced a bill calling for 'Free and Compulsory Primary Education' in the state in such areas as required it at the discretion of the Government, and in his constituency of Mattancherry.[31]

He got the support of fellow legislator Sahodaran Ayyappan. However, Rao Sahib I. N. Menon, who was Director of Public In-struction, opposed it - arguing that 'the sinews of war did not per-mit the acceptance of the resolution.'

It took another six years before another member Kumaran Ezhuthassan introduced the Cochin Free Compulsory Primary Education Bill on August 13, 1947 - which was cleared by a select

30 *Viswakarmas* is a social group in Kerala comprised mainly of trade artisans/crafts-men like carpenters, goldsmiths, masons, blacksmiths, goldsmiths and bronzesmiths. Hindu legend says they are descended from Vishwakarma who was the divine engineer and architect of the entire universe.

31 Kochukrishnan R, *"Sahodharan Ayyappan and the Socio-Political Movement in Kerala"*, University of Kerala Thesis, 2012, pg 213.

committee a couple of days before Indian independence. The bill got royal assent on March 12, 1948.[32]

•••••

ON THE CONSTITUTION OF NEW TOWN COUNCILS

A. B. Salem : May I know whether any one individual member sitting on the Treasury Bench is responsible for such communication (about new councils)?

•••••

ON THE ISSUE OF LACK OF INFORMATION ON BUYING ELECTRICITY FROM PALIVASAL PROJECT IN TRAVANCORE[33]

A. B. Salem: Has the information not been given publicly in the Travancore Council?

A. B. Salem: May I know, Sir, whether you will be good enough to include the coastal areas as well, Chellanam, Pallippuram, etc.? - in addition to Trichur area, Chowwarra, Chennamangalam-Paravur border and Edapalli frontier?

•••••

THE QUESTION OF LEVY OF TOLLS IN THE PORT AREA

A. B. Salem: Will the Government be pleased to state (a) whether they have authorised the establishment of an out-post at the entrance of the Port area outside the walls in the vicinity of the road-bridge approach and the Mattancheri Halt Station where a collection of 8 *annas* is made on every car entering the port limits, to go past it to the Harbour area or to the Harbour Terminus Railway Station;

(b) under what authority or provision of law is this levy of 8 annas on every car entering the Port area, made; and the Railway Station, and if so, how this right is curtailed by the levy of 8 annas on cars;

(c) if the levy is not made with the sanction of the Cochin Government, will the Government be pleased to state under whose

---

32 Ibid.

33 The Palivasal Project was the first hydro-electric project in Kerala in the mountainous Idukki district, commissioned in 1940, during the reign of Maharaja Sree Chithira Thirunal Balarama Varma of Travancore, and inaugurated by Sir C P Ramaswamy Aiyer, then Diwan of Travancore.

authority and under what provision of law is this levy made;

(d) whether this levy of 8 *annas* is made with the sanction of the Harbour Advisory Committee and whether the levy has been publicly notified in the *Cochin Government Gazette* or otherwise;

(e) whether such levy is made in other major ports in India where Port Trusts exist to administer their affairs;

(f) whether the public have right of way on the roads within the Port area to proceed to the public offices and the Railway Stations;

(g) whether rickshaws or other vehicles are also to pay anything for entering into the Port area roads?

A. B. Salem: Are you entitled to levy this charge?

When pointed out that the Port Area was private property:

A. B. Salem: Then your consent or knowledge is not necessary?

A. B. Salem: Is it your case that in the Port area anything can be done by the Port Authorities?

A. B. Salem ...Suppose in a private land you have got a right of way. Is the owner entitled to levy a toll?

A. B. Salem: Before the Government gave the consent did they find out whether it will be legal or illegal? What was the hurry to levy this before a law was passed?

A. B. Salem: May I know where the Railway station is? Have not the people going to the Railway station to pass through this illegal levy station?

Advocate-General M. Sivarama Menon intervenes to say that the railway station was inside the Port area.

A. B. Salem: To go to the Railway station, the public have to pass through this illegal levy post. Is the Government aware that the public have to go there? Is there any Act either by the Government of India or by the Cochin Government with regard to this road? How was this consent given without the authority of an Act? No pie *(the lowest monetary unit)* can be taken from the public without a law. Was not the Government aware of this elementary principle? Does the Government think that only consent was necessary to levy a toll? The question was whether the legality or otherwise was examined before you gave your consent?

A Government Minister then pointed out that legislation would be passed in regard to the toll.

A. B. Salem: Am I to understand that these tolls on the public road which you mentioned in (f) are imposed without an Act or Regulation but only by consent and knowledge? May I know whether it is the usual practice when such levies are imposed to publish them in the *Cochin Government Gazette*? Can the Hon'ble Joint Secretary point but one single instance where any tax has been imposed without publishing it in the Gazette?

•••••

TENANCY LAW IN THE HARBOUR AREA

A. B. Salem: Is there no Tenancy Law equally applicable to the area under the jurisdiction of the Port Authorities? '

The Government replies that the Port Area was exempted.

•••••

HARBOUR WORKS-RECRUITMENT OF LABOUR RULES

A. B. Salem: Will Government be pleased to state:

(a) in recruiting ordinary labour, is there any rule or practice or custom followed in the Harbour Works;

(b) if so, what;

(c) is the Government aware that men who have worked long years in the Harbour are thrown out and sometimes preference given to new recruits?

P. V. Raphael Joint Secretary to Government replies that the Government has no information. This infuriates Salem.

A. B. Salem: Did the Government call for information? Is the welfare of the people working in the Harbour not a matter of importance to Government? Is not the Government of Cochin a responsible government to whom we are putting questions? Are you not partners in the Harbour?

A. B. Salem: I want to know whether there is any rule of practise with regard to the labour, because it affects a large number of people in my constituency.

People are coming to me and complaining that they are being sent out, people who have got 13 or 14 years of work to their credit are simply turned out without reason. These are the things that will bring revolution in the country. People are starving. People with 4 to 5 children to maintain, after 15 or 18 years of hard work in the Harbour, going into mud, going into water and losing their health, are simply asked to go away and favourites are put in their places. That is the complaint. Therefore, I ask whether there is a practice or custom followed.

Other members join in the grilling of the government official.

A. B. Salem: Now that the Government has heard complaints in this House, will the Government be pleased to either to make an enquiry into the matter, whether the welfare of the citizens of Cochin is well cared, or whether they are ill-treated, or maltreated or well-treated?

The welfare of the masses is your first concern. In the first concern, you do not ask for the information. I can't understand it.

The government assures that the issue will be looked into and see that the interests of the Cochin labourers are safeguarded.

•••••

DURING A DEBATE ON GRANTS

Salem kept haranguing in the council for more powers to be delegated to members to make decisions and not just be an advisory body. He spoke about this autonomy during most debates - even if it was as mundane as sanctioning of grants. This demand for more responsibility was getting shriller after each session of the council.

A. B. Salem: Sir, the question of responsible government for our State is a matter that is very near to my heart. I have been raising my voice and fighting for the establishment of responsible government in Cochin from the very day this Council was constituted and even before that.

I maintain, Sir, that with all the defects that we have in Cochin amidst our people we are nevertheless more than fit for the exercise of responsibility when responsible government is given to us. If, in British India, in Madras, Bombay and all the other provinces - they could have full provincial autonomy, with less average intelligence and education, then in Cochin, I can see no reason whatsoever to deny the more advanced people of Cochin that which is given in British India. I have seen the Councils of Bombay, Bengal and Madras Provinces sitting.

C. V. Iyyu: Have you seen the Parliament sitting?

A. B. Salem: No. No. When you examine Parliament. I shall speak about that. If you have got something sensible you can interrupt *(Hear, hear) (Laughter)*.

When you see them working there, no doubt, you will find not more than five or six outstanding figures in those legislatures. But the average is much less than the average we have got in our Council. When the play of vote comes it may be that the very best of our men may not come here. That does not matter. That will be only in the beginning of things. And voters, after a few exercise of the votes, will come to realize that it is their duty and it is for their benefit alone that they should send the best men available in the country to the Council.

Parties will rise and fall, but the exercise of responsibility is the only way to get the sense of responsibility developed. So long as you make us irresponsible critics who have got nothing to shoulder, who have got no chance of ousting the members seated as part of the Government and taking their place, so long as they are irremovable and we are only mere critics, we cannot develop that sense of responsibility.

Take, for instance, the case of our most virulent member whom our late Diwan has even characterized as a tiger when he was here in this side. How nice he has become when responsibility was given to him! Although at times his anger we are able to feel here, how calm and cool he has become with the shouldering of responsibility!

It is not a mere question of saying that we must show our fitness. How can we show our fitness? Give us the purse. Do you ever question the character, integrity or ability and the capacity of all officers of the Government who are recruited from amongst us? Several officers that are seated here are competent; eminent gentlemen of character and standing. Is there a single voice against the officers of the public service of Cochin, or its judiciary or its executive? No doubt, in appointments sometimes the choice of their appointees may be a matter of difference of opinion.

But, nevertheless, every man appointed is found to be absolutely competent: Who could dare say that our Rama Varma Thampuran, Finance Member is not competent? No doubt, I must say that he would not have become Finance Member but for the fact that he is the Prince. But they are all different matters.

What we are concerned with here is whether he has got all qualities, abilities and capacities. By this what I mean to say is everybody should be given equal opportunities to prove their worth. That was what I wanted to say the other day. But I was not allowed to say that (*Laughter*).

Let a Civil Service examination come. Apart from that our capacity, I say has been testified; '[Some] Years ago Bishop Whitehead, the Metropolitan of Madras;[34] who visited Cochin said, "If there is any piece of ground or area in the whole of India where the experiment of responsible government can be tried without any fear of any mishap, that area is Cochin State."

If after 30-40 years since then if anyone says that our fitness must be 'again tested, I say that is a proposition that will not hold any water. If the 1935 Act can be passed for the Government of India - and six years have rolled by after that in the Provinces - I ask, what justification have you to deny the advanced State of Cochin the privilege of responsible government?

After all, what is responsible government in India? The Indian responsible government, for a long time, will be only a protected government... both in British India and in the Native States of India. Is the British Government going to go bag and baggage from India? Is the defence of India going to be given up? I don't think that these things are going to be, even during our children's time.

I would also like to see it. But it is not a possible thing, it is not a practical thing for the present when there are guns, howitzers, bombs and bombers of which you have no idea. What is it that has happened during the last 150 years in India? We have been emasculated completely.

Salem is asked here by the Council President to cut short his rambling speech.

A. B. Salem: Sir, the grant of full responsible government has been conceded by His Highness when the Government of Cochin Act was passed in 1113. Four years have practically rolled by since and I think we were content with it, because there were other con-

---

34 Henry Whitehead (1853–1947) was an Anglican priest who was Bishop of Madras for 23 years, from 1899 to 1922. He is the author of the book 'The Village Gods of South India', published in 1916.

siderations which weighed with us when we accepted this diarchi-
cal form of government.

It is not a thing we liked... But we accepted what has been given
by His Highness out of his own free will. But now what has been
given by the right hand in the Government of Cochin Act has been
taken away with the left by way of rules. Therefore, what I submit
is, His Highness can depend upon his loyal and devoted subjects to
do that which is right by His Highness and by the people of Cochin.

Impose trust in us and trust will beget trust. Give us responsibility and we will act responsibly and in the best interests of the
people of Cochin.

The patriots of Cochin will feel well in the new regime of His
Highness Sri Kerala Varma if His Highness will grant us full responsible government; in other words we want His Highness to
rest upon the love and devotion of his own people more than on
the protection of even bayonets of others. This love of the people
demands trust in the people. If responsible government is given
us, we will respond splendidly, both in loyalty and ability and in
capacity and in looking after the welfare of the people of Cochin.

•••••

CUT MOTION NO.4

To reduce the allotment of Rs 1,44,387 for General Administration by Rs. 3 (To urge the adoption of the salutary policy of making
salaries of the officers in the Transferred Departments Votable by
this House).

A. B. Salem: Sir, my motion is to reduce the allotment of Rs
1,44,387 for General Administration by Rs. 3. This cut is for the
purpose of urging the adoption of the salutary policy of making
salaries of the officers in the Transferred Departments Votable by
this House.

Now, Sir, about 8 departments have been transferred to the
charge of the Hon'ble Minister. What is it that we are aiming at by
transfer? What is the use of simply transferring a few departments
to the Minister? That which used to be done in a particular way
before is to be done in another way now...

What is the transfer that we are asking for? The control over these departments was that of an irresponsible Diwan before and the control of these departments have been transferred from 'irresponsible Diwan[35]' to 'the Minister who is responsible' to this House so that these departments have passed from the realms of irresponsibility to the realms of responsibility.

Now if any officer in the Transferred Department is not put under the control of the Minister and the control of this House, what is the transfer that has been effected? It is futile. They will get their usual salary without any difficulty. There is no transfer of power in reality to this House or to the Minister. Therefore, every officer in the Transferred Departments should come within the control of this House and how can this House exercise control?

Only by voting the salary of these officers. If by virtue of section 28 (e) you keep the appointments of the officers in the Transferred Departments outside the purview of this House in spite of the transfer of control from the irresponsible realms of the Diwan to the responsible realms of the Minister, and if those appointments are not to be even considered by this House, I say your reform is a sham, a pretence - a mass of pretences and nothing more.

Therefore it is incumbent on our part to strengthen our own hands by fighting for our rights which they apparently want to make the world believe that they are Transferred Departments. Let us face realities.

Now you have transferred 8 departments but not a single officer can be fined or dealt with in any manner. His salary is beyond the vote of this House, We cannot even censure him. Our Minister also cannot do It. If that be so, what is the inherent worth of these masses of pretences in the Constitution Act?

Government is in the shape of diarchy here. It is better that we do not have this costly paraphernalia of a Legislative Council and a Minister if, in reality, you want to do and continue to do as you please. Sir, I can very well understand the anxiety on the part of the framers of the Constitution Act that the Civil Services in a country must be kept free from molestation and must be made secure in their services.

If every Member of this House is to have a finger in the pie, in

---

35 The Diwan at the time was R. K. Shanmukham Chetty.

their salary and cut them, they may not be free to carry on their administration. And the political nature of this house will reflect itself in the department and the departmental heads may not be doing their duty, but may be running with the party in power.

That anxiety I can very well understand. The civil service in any country must be kept in a way that they must carry out the wishes of the Ministry in power - those who pay them, whoever they may be. They have to carry out their policy, whatever it may be and to carry it out loyally.

They should not have any hand in the shaping of the policy. If they go against it and if we are dissatisfied with the control exercised by the Minister over the civil services, we do not touch the civil service, but deal with the estimates that the · Minister brings before us for our scrutiny and we cut them.

Here what could we cut? He is not responsible for it. The whole thing is put in italics. Even the officers whose salaries have been votable have been transferred back into the non-votable category. Our progress, instead of going forward, has been retrogressive and going backward. If that is the policy you are going to adopt, then I say, the sooner you do away with that policy, the better it is for all concerned. Because there has been an increase in the salary a votable item became non-votable.

That is not a good position for the Government to take up -increase the salary to any man and then make it non-votable. I have no case against increasing the salary.

It depends on merit; but my point is, it must still remain in the votable realms where it was. The power of the Council should not have been touched at all.

Therefore I submit that the salaries of all the officers in the Transferred Departments must be put in the votable part of the budget. I press this issue. I will press the motion to a division because it is a salutary policy to make the salaries of officers in the Transferred Departments votable by this House.

A. B. Salem: I thank the Chair for its generosity, for the opportunity that is given me so that our voices will be known. I am sure the Government of His Highness will consider the matter. I don't want to press the motion to a division. But I would like to know what the view of the Government on the point is.

The Council President points out that the Constitution Act makes provision for such points.

A. B. Salem: Because this is a matter that goes against the provisions of the Act I do not wish to have any further discussion on it. I therefore beg leave of the House to withdraw my motion...

The issue is put to rest.

CUT MOTION NO. 7
STOCKING AND CONTROLLING THE PRICE OF RICE.

(Salem was one of the few council members who raised their voices against hoarding and profiteering by wealthy traders - and made recommendations that included the levying of a super tax on obscene profits - these statements remain as relevant today as it was in the early 19th century.

(A paragraph of his speech here reads: "Sir, if you just cross the ferry you will find the misery there - a number of little children with mere skin and bone - a number of women in tatters sleeping in verandahs of buildings - a most heart-rending and miserable sight!")

.....

A. B. Salem: Sir, I rise to move to reduce the allotment of Rs. 1,44,387 for General Administration by Re. 1 to urge the immediate need of adopting a policy of keeping a sufficient stock of rice under Government control, to keep down and control the price of rice to help the people of Cochin.

Sir, whenever Governments want to shelve any matter, the usual policy adopted not only by our Government but by all Governments is to appoint a committee. With the appointment of the committee the responsibility of the Government ceases and the Government can put up their hand and say: 'We have appointed a committee with a non-official majority and if they agree we are quite prepared', and this poor committee will not know what to do. Generally that is the trouble. If people who are in the Government service and who have got power do not know how to do, how will this poor committee of people with no exercise of responsibility and power be able to do?

What is it to be done? Our people are suffering, and are we going to look after it and doing anything? Here is the rice, the cost of which has gone from Rs. 7 to Rs. 12-8-0. Take the case of a peon who gets Rs. 10 or Rs. 15. With Rs, 7 for a bag he was managing his house. With Rs. 2, he will purchase other things. Now the price has gone up to Rs. 12-8-0. That means he cannot have a bag of rice in his house. That is the position.

So my case is that the Government in such a situation and emergency must come to the help of the masses for whom they profess their sympathies always. We are here always to look after the masses. Every big man's statement is: 'My sympathy to the poor is unbounded'. But when it actually comes to the working of that sympathy into some tangible thing like giving them rice, then the sympathies vanish in the air. Such a situation should be avoided and that is the object of this motion.

I ask the Government to keep a stock of a lakh of bags always with them which they can sell at Rs, 7 or Rs. 8. You will ask how? I say: Sir, if you will only have a bold policy. the power is with the Government to take rice from every godown, stock it in a central place. Was it not done during the last war? Was there not a central depot run by the Government during the last war? It was a great boon to the people. Never mind we may lose 2 lakhs, 3 lakhs, or 5 lakhs of rupees.

Where is it going? Into the stomachs of the poorest of the poor people. Be liberal. This is the time when you should come to the financial help of the great masses for whom you always profess your sympathies.

That is the point. I would even ask the Government if in this emergency, the Government feel the necessity for financing this stock of rice, impose a special tax upon those who have been selling rice and profiting, a special rice tax upon rice merchants, whose income may come to a certain limit.

Replying to a question about rice merchants resorting to an increase in price, Salem replies: If they are having a proift of Rs. 50,000 and above, take 50 per cent of the money from them. By buying rice and selling it at a cheaper rate, we will be suffering a loss. This is a situation in which we must buy rice at a higher price and sell it at a lower price. The usual course is to buy at a lower price and sell at a higher price. But now you should buy at a higher price and sell to the poor at a lower price and recoup the loss from those who have profited by the sale of this very rice in the country. Sir, I will tell you the merchants have been getting rice at Rs. 8. They have stocked it at Rs. 8. They must be asked to sell at that price, plus ordinary profit.

The nominated Jewish member in the Council S S. Koder, who is also a leading merchant, asks: But when the prices go down?

A. B. Salem: Then they will suffer a little loss. It is only during emergency time. This is not the policy that the Government should adopt always. When a situation like that comes you must meet the situation by extraordinary measures.

What is the situation in England? In any man's private house they can compel anybody to be given accommodation and allowed to sleep there. Nobody can say: 'It is my private house, my own property, I have no room here to give...'

Here, Salem was referring to the World War II years.

Emergency laws have been passed. If the Government officers come and say, 'Give that bedroom to him', you have to. That is the situation with which they are faced. Food is controlled there. That is why we asked the Government to come in.

When Mr. Banerji came here, he said there were plenty of people in England who were not willing to house all kinds of people, and Government officers would go there, wipe away their objections and do what is needed for the country. People's houses are broken; bombs have been falling upon their houses. They are in the street. They cannot sleep in the cold and you say .... I want to be cosy and comfortable in my own house. I won't admit anybody".

Such a situation demands this, because they are charged with the welfare of the people of the land. Similarly, although you have not such a duty cast upon you by force of public opinion and by responsibility to this House, they are your own people, every one of you knows their difficulties. Look at the distribution of rice near Krishna Vilas Palace. Why is His Highness distributing rice? Why does my friend Mr. Popatlal distribute rice to the people of Mattancherri?

Member C. V. Iyyu from Kunnankulam, who always pokes Salem with sarcastic one-liners says: Because he is afraid of looting.

A. B. Salem: There is no looting as in Kunnamkulam where the people grudge to pay the Town Council tax. How far can one single merchant or two do? As regards the rice merchants in Mattancheri you need have no consideration, because most of them have come only for the purpose of making money. They have not got any special relationship in the land, except to make as much money as they can and to pay as little as possible when they cannot withstand the demand.

Have a supertax after Rs. 50,000. Fifty per cent of the profit should be taken from them during this emergency time. That is what I insist upon. I know I may be unpopular among my merchant friends. But that does not matter. It is the masses that have to be considered, and it is in their interest that I am urging the keeping of a central depot and keeping a large stock and financing it in the ways that I have already stated.

Let Government give a contribution by a special rice tax. Upon whom will it fall? Upon the very big people who can afford to pay that. After Rs. 50.000 profit, they should pay a tax. Sir. if you just cross the ferry you will find the misery there - a number of little children with mere skin and bone - a number of women in tatters sleeping in verandahs of buildings - a most heart-rending and miserable sight! Are we to see this? Unfortunately, I have no money. Otherwise, I would have given them money. I can freely talk.

Another member from Mattancheri, Ismail Hajee Essa Sait, who is on the Food Committee, flares up: "That is why you are saying this..."

A. B. Salem retorts: You have got plenty of money. Give half of it. Let the poor eat. It will come back to you. You have got enough of land, enough of property, enough of coconuts. Feed the poor. [Sait is on the committee]...that is one of the reasons that nothing will be done by the committee.

Therefore, Sir. I urge that the Government would kindly, graciously accept this resolution to keep a rice stock. The quantity that you should keep etc. are all matters of detail that you can regulate. I say, if you keep at least one lakh of bags or rice, the prices will regulate themselves. If rice is sold at Rs. 10 we can begin to sell at Rs. 7. If our stock is exhausted, we can commandeer what the merchants have got and fill our stock. How to finance? By taxing the profit over Rs. 50,000. Therefore, I commend this motion to the acceptance of this House.

At this juncture, **Mr. Iyyu** says members of the Food Control Committee were laughing at A.B. Salem. Iyyu points out that the committee comprises wealthy members like V. K. Bhaskara Menon who gets several hundreds of thousands para of rice[36] from his vast paddy fields, Khan Sahib Ismail Hajee Essa Seit, S. S. Koder and Govind Pai who are interested parties in the debate. These are people who have not understood what poverty means. So I suggest that this committee be disbanded and other people appointed to it. I support Salem's motion.

N. Govinda Pai and **Ismail Seit** put forward arguments against the motion, saying "there is enough stock of rice... if we stock it, it will deteriorate... merchants are fair people and regulate themselves etc."

The Council decided to follow up on the issue and the motion was put forward and carried.

•••••

Debate of 5th December 1944, in the Council Hall, Ernakulam, with Sir George Boag, K.C.I.E., C.S.I. in the Chair

A. B. Salem raised several minor points during this session, including the export of milch cattle to British Madras, processing of sweet toddy and the manufacture of jaggery[37], arrangement for husking paddy and the shortage of grazing land in his constituency of Mattancherry.

The alleged hoarding and shortage of fountain pens in Cochin also raised Salem's ire. "Are [members] aware that in Madras, per-

---

36 *Para* - a measuring vessel used in Kerala's rice trading system. One *para* is equivalent to about 8 kilograms.

37 Jaggery is cane sugar without separation of the molasses and crystals.

mits are necessary to buy or sell fountain pens?" he bellowed.

(Blogger Abraham Tharakan has reminisced about this issue: "There were problems for students in the Cochin Kingdom...in the 1940s...Writing instruments like Waterman's and Swan pens and 'Aana (elephant) mark' (German made Staedler) pencils disappeared from the market. The local substitutes scratched along the paper...)[38]

He also spoke briefly about the price of rice in Karachi and the possibility of importing it to Cochin. He did not make substantive or long speeches on any other subject.

•••••
MONDAY THE 15TH JANUARY 1945
The Council met in the Council Hall, Ernakulam, at half past Eleven of the Clock with the Hon'ble the President (Sir George Boag, K.C.I.E., C.S.I - who was Diwan of Cochin from 1943-1944) in the Chair.

On Purchase and Repair of Furniture - Huzoor Secretariat

A. B. Salem: Sir, I think the ante-room before you get into the Diwan's room may be converted into a visitors' room. There are a number of chairs kept on the verandah. (*A voice: "How many"*?) More than six.

The difficulties are more than exaggerated. A number of chairs arc there. Certainly it will add dignity to the Secretariat to have a proper ante-room. I am one with you there and also I think it is only right that whatever be the conditions, war conditions or other conditions, the Secretariat must be kept spick-and-span and most attractively and most beautifully and at least some varnish will be good and very usefully spent.

I always thought that the only officer who has an eye for all these things is Mr. Mathew. His room is always very neat and tidy. 1 do not know how he manages it. As regards the other places, they are not as well kept, as it ought to be. The suggestion may be considered.

---

38 Tharakan Abraham: *Some memories of WW II, Cochin* http://abrahamtharakanblog. blogspot.ca/2007_01_01_archive.html

Debate on ADJOURNMENT MOTION 'On the indifference shown in the preparation of the Preliminary Electoral Roll'

A. B. Salem: The preparation of the list is the first item in the elections and it is the duty of the Government and of this House to see that the list is prepared as perfectly as possible in the preliminary stage. Corrections and additions can come afterwards.

Very stringent rules have been laid down for the preparation of the list because that is the rock bottom in which the whole edifice rests. The right of franchise is a very valuable right and it should not be defeated in any way by any officer concerned.

Rules relating to this matter of franchise are laid down on page 109 of the Government of Cochin Act. That is rule 7. An electoral roll shall be prepared for every constituency on which shall be entered the names of all persons *prima facie* entitled to be registered as electors for that constituency. It shall be published in the Gazette. Why is it published in the Gazette? So that it may have the widest possible publicity.

Under the conditions that the war has brought about we have dispensed with that and, therefore, the widest publicity is restricted at this time. Therefore, all the more vigilance must be bestowed in the preparation of the list.

The next important rule regarding the preparation of the electoral roll is rule 4 on page 132. A person 'shall be qualified as an elector for a General Constituency who is a *pattadar*, etc., (a) to (g). It includes all those persons who are taxed either in the Municipality or who pays any land 'tax out-side or a fishing stakes tax or any tax whatsoever. As for the tax-payers there is no difficulty. There is no difficulty to my mind to find it out. Tax-payers' list is from time to time an annual list. The tax collecting officers have that list. That list may *ipso facto* be copied from the various circles where the lists are prepared.

One other rule comes in here that is regarding (g). Anyone who has passed the School Final Examination (declared eligible for Public Service or College Admission or both) or its equivalents such as the Cambridge Senior or the Matriculation or the Oriental Titles Examination or Sanskrit Pandit's examination and such other tests as may, from time to time, be prescribed by the Government in this behalf. That is the extension, of the franchise.

Franchise went beyond the payment of money and recognized intellectuals...

Now that is a very important matter. As already sufficiently pointed out a person who has once passed these examinations can never be disqualified. A person who has been paying tax in a year may not be paying tax in the next year, but a person who has passed the School Final is always a School Final, till his death.

Once he goes into the list there is no justification of any kind to remove that man from that particular list unless death is established or some other disqualification by which his name must go from the roll.

It cannot be pleaded as a mitigating circumstance that the officers concerned had other work to do, that the time available has been so short and that it has been done in a very hurried fashion. I would, therefore, request the Government that the best may be done to make the list as perfect as can possibly be under the circumstances now obtaining.

I say that in preparing the preliminary electoral roll we have got these data which are Government data for which you have not to go outside the Department. Then the other rule is rule 6 (a) at page 06 which says about the preparation of the electoral rolls by the Registration Officer. The duties of the Registration Officer must be performed by his deputy. Then there is one other rule. That Is rule 09 on page 139. The Registration Officer may, of his own motion, remove from the rolls the names of persons whom he has reason to believe to be dead and may make such other corrections as may be necessary.

Then there is Rule J6 on page 140. The Returning Officers and the Registration Officers shall keep copies of the rolls or Parts 01 rolls and the lists of additions and corrections ... in their offices and for supply to the presiding officers at the polls.

The word additions is only there. In all other places it is correction. The law has contemplated the possibility of additions in a matter like this. This is a fit case in which that power should be exercised. If the Government comes to the conclusion that the lists have not been prepared happily, I will not go beyond that. Get it corrected.

It is seen that the Diwan's name or the acting Diwan's name is not there. It is scandalous to have such names omitted. Therefore, the time has come and the reasons have been established for an additional list of voters to be prepared. The Registration Officer has the power to do that and there is no difficulty. Names of persons who have passed the School Final Examinations have to be added. Now persons with educational qualifications are not given the power of voting by removing their names. It would be a shame to stand and look on for correcting such a position. Therefore, I would request you to see that the list of additions is prepared and published . . . It is not too late.

Only on the 13th the Revising Authorities have been asked to finish their work. It is not very late. In 10 days' time it can be finished. After all, the Cochin State is very small. It consists of 279 villages and you have got 279 *Parvathiams*.[39]

I would, therefore, suggest to the Government to take expeditious steps kindly to see such a scandalous state of affairs is not made the basis of the election even in war time. What is going to come? We want election. But we must go through the procedure correctly and properly.

There are cases in which the names of persons have been purposely omitted at the instance of candidates. If somehow the date fixed for putting the claim is passed, his name will not be there and he will have to look up to the stars. Is such a thing to be tolerated by the Government or by those in authority or in charge of the preparation of the lists?

Therefore, it is suggested that the preliminary roll shall be prepared as correctly as possible. I, therefore, think that I have shown sufficient and given constructive suggestions to the Government to get over the difficulty. The list of additions and corrections may be ordered to be made.

You have done away with the publication in the Gazette. Pub-

---

39 The Kingdom's villages had Headmen or *Pramanakkars* who were appointed by the Government and worked with officials who were called *Parvathiams*.

licity is not there. What is the difficulty in making the list of additions? There is absolutely no difficulty. It is much better to do that than deprive people of their franchise that the law has given them. Certainly the technicality is there. It can be used this way and the other way.

So apart from technicalities, the heavens are not going to fall down if one week's time is allowed. In the time we have got, we shall have the thing done. There is no great hurry.

Elections are to come only in *Edavam* (May-June, according to the Malayalam calendar[40]). We have only to prepare the list of additions. Have it revised and added to the list. What is the difficulty?

A. V. Moothedan, the member from Chalakkudi, points out that village clerks, when entering names in the electoral rolls, make glaring errors. *"In Malayalam, Mathunni is written as Chathunni, with the result that a Christian become an Ezhava."* The names of persons who are well-known in society... are omitted.

The Government then assures the Council that action will be taken to correct names if they are pointed out to officials.

• • • • •

Author T. C. Narayan tells a story in his book *'Ettukettu Stories'* about A. B. Salem resorting to drama - after all, he was the agitator and main debater in the Council chambers. Salem apparently had a bitter argument with the then Diwan of Cochin... on some funding demands for his Mattancherry constituency. The annoyed Diwan admonished Salem and asked him to go and 'beg' for assistance outside the assembly hall.

That evening Salem appeared at the gates of the Diwan's house, dressed in a beggar's rags and carrying a bowl and stick and sent word through the guards to the Diwan that he was following his advice and seeking handouts.[41]

• • • • •

Another incident told by Ruby Daniel describes how Salem used to arrange *kosher* food for Cochin Assembly members whenever there was a state banquet - and there were many members who

---

40 The Malayalam Calendar or Kollam Era is a solar Hindu calendar based on constellations and fixed stars. The origin of the calendar in Kerala has been dated as 825 AD.

41 Narayaan T.C. *Ettukettu Stories*, pg 116.

loved the Jewish fare.

Before one such dinner - during his second term in the assembly - Salem requested Jew Town families to provide him with fifty *kippas* (Jewish skull caps). The women stitched the caps and Salem took it to the Council. When all members were seated around the dinner table, Salem took out a cap from his bag and fixed it on his head. He then took out another cap and put it on the head of Diwan Shanmukham Chetty[42].

Soon, everyone was clamouring for one and 50 members of the council began dinner with Jewish caps on their heads. Ruby wrote: "...one of the members called out and said, 'When Tipu Sultan wanted to convert Hindus to Islam he had to send his soldiers with a cap in one hand and a sword in the other...

'Either the cap on your head or your head in the cap...' So out of fear, many Hindus converted to Islam. But when Mr. Salem wanted fifty people to put on the cap, he managed it without instilling the fear of death."[43]

---

42 Diwan Chetty was the powerful prime minister of Cochin from 1935 to 1941.

43 Ruby and Johnson, *Ruby of Cochin*, pg 140.

CHAPTER VIII

Salem, Zionism & The Aliyah

From the hoary days of Jewish settlement in the Kingdom of Cochin, the toast in every Jewish home was *L'Shana Haba'ah B'Yerushalayim* ('Next Year in Jerusalem'). It was more like an Utopian dream, as it was for the Jewish diaspora worldwide before the horrors of the Second World War and the birth of Israel.

David Ben-Gurion, Executive Head of the World Zionist Organization and Chairman of the Jewish Agency for Palestine, proclaimed the establishment of the State of Israel on May 14, 1948. The *Aliyah* or the Ingathering of Exiles began in earnest.

The proclamation stated: 'The State of Israel will be open for Jewish immigration from all countries of their dispersion...WE APPEAL to the Jewish people throughout the Diaspora to rally round the Jews of Eretz-Israel in the tasks of immigration and upbuilding and to stand by them in the great struggle for the realization of the age-old dream - the redemption of Israel...'[1]

This was followed by the Law of Return, promulgated on July 5, 1950 which declared: 'Every Jew has the right to come to this country as an *oleh* (immigrant).' The law also specified that applicants can be denied citizenship if they have an illness which could

---

[1] Israel Ministry of Foreign Affairs, *Declaration of Establishment of State of Israel*, https://mfa.gov.il/mfa.

pose a serious public health risk to the people of Israel.[2]

The Zionist dream took roots in Cochin at the turn of the 20th century with a Paradesi Jew Napthali Roby writing to Jewish leader Theodore Herzl[3] about Zionism and the need to start a movement in India and collect funds for the same.

No formal organizations were set up in Cochin until 1930, when societies were formed mainly to press for educational and other benefits from the government. Among them were the Malabar Jews Association, the Cochin Zionist Association, the Habonim (a Zionist youth group), and the Malabar Zionist Movement.

The Koder family established the Malabar Jews Association in 1932 with Samuel Koder as President and son Shabtai Koder as Secretary and Treasurer; Salem was appointed Vice-President[4] and stayed on until it was dissolved in 1947. Salem was also the Secretary of the Cochin Zionist Association.

The elder Koder was the sponsor of the Habonim. Ruby Daniel says everybody called it Gedud Shingly or the Shingly Battalion, in honour of the original Jewish settlement of Cranganore. Jack Japheth, a Baghdadi Jew from Bombay, frequently visited Cochin and taught rousing Hebrew songs to the youngsters.[5]

When the then Governor-General of India, Lord Louis Mountbatten accompanied by Lady Edwina Mountbatten visited Cochin in February/March 1948, a Habonim contingent presented a guard of honour for the couple in front of the Paradesi Synagogue.

On May 14 that year, there was rejoicing in all synagogues in Cochin to mark the declaration of Israeli independence, with the most exuberant event at Mattancherry, under the aegis of Salem, Koder and other community leaders. A spontaneous Simchat Tora celebration was organized with the Sefer Torah taken around the synagogue in procession, with music, dance and feasting thereafter. (*Simchat Torah is a joyous holiday that celebrates the Jewish love of*

---

2 *The Law of Return 5710 (1950)*, https://knesset.gov.il/laws

3 Theodor Herzl (1860-1904) was an Austro-Hungarin Jew who is known as the father of modern political Zionism. In 1896, he called for the settlement of Jews in their ancient homeland.

4 Cited by Prof. Chiriyinkandath, various sources.

5 Daniel and Johnson, *Ruby of Cochin*, pg 93.

Torah and in 1948, the regular celebration was in October).

From 1951 to 1954, Salem served as Chair of the Board of Trustees for the United Synagogues of Malabar, which was disbanded after most of the Malabari Jews left for Israel.

•••••

After failing to get elected in the second Cochin Legislative Assembly, in the early 1930s, Salem began delving into Zionism. Salem's mother Belukka had died in December 1929 when he was in Lahore attending the famous session of the Indian National Congress (1929-1930), where the first declaration for Indian Independence was made. In 1933, he made the difficult journey to Palestine (where he stayed for five months) - and interred the remains of his mother on the Mount of Olives in Jerusalem.[6]

Salem was the first prominent Cochin Jew to have visited Palestine, before the birth of Israel and to have recorded his visit. *(The only other Cochin Jewish person said to have visited Palestine was a Malabari Jew named Eliya Madai in 1903.)*[7]

Salem's idealized image of Palestine, like most Jews in Cochin, was that of a land 'flowing with milk and honey, as a land for the bearded and as a land where one can find the right place to worship God'. He noted his observations on Palestine in his dairy and was put off with the lifestyle of the Arabs and the wretched conditions they lived in.

He wrote: "...walked out into old Jerusalem – into the labyrinthine part inhabited by Arabs and saw their poor life in all its squalor, filth and crowd . . . she [his guide] then took me to a peasant's stone hole... a pregnant Arab woman, her blind husband, a child with measles . . . were warming their fingers by the side of the hillside house . . . fire in a square pot or tin receptacle – OK! What poor & hard life!"[8]

While he found squalor in the Arab quarters, he was impressed

---

6 The Jewish Cemetery on the Mount of Olives is the most ancient cemetery in Jerusalem, where burial began 3,000 years ago in the time of the First Temple.

7 Cited by Johnson, Barbara, *Our Community in Two Worlds*, PhD Thesis, 1985 - pg 89 - from Ben Eliyahu, ed. *The Jews of Malabar White and Black, Ernakulam,* Indo-Israel Publications, 1966.

8 Salem's Diary No. 5, February, 1933: *Travels in Palestine - Bethlehem and Hebron* - at Magnes, Entry of April 1, 1933. Cited by Prof. Chiriyinkandath.

with the development in other areas. In an article that he wrote after returning to Cochin, he said he found that 'everything there was being carried on the principles of the West', because of the excellent work being done by the Halutzim and Haluzmoth (Hebrew, *men and women pioneers*).[9]

He wrote in his diary that he attended a ball at King David Hotel[10] and the eighth anniversary gala of Hebrew University to hear speeches by Chaim Weizmann (who later became president of Israel) and Professor Judah Magnes (founder, Chancellor and later President of Hebrew University).

He held discussions with both Zionist and Arab businessmen and procured a Palestine Immigration Certificate for his family (although he had no plans to emigrate!). He also floated an Indo-Palestine Company in Cochin to engage in the export and import trade, but that did not take off.

As a leader of the Cochin Jews, Salem was in constant contact with Zionist leaders in Palestine through letters and telegrams. He also sent frequent reports about politics to Leo Herman of the Keren Hayesod (The Foundation Fund)[11] of the Jewish Agency and sought funds to set up an information office in Cochin.

One tragedy that shook him was the assassination in 1933 of one of his ideological brothers, Haim (Victor) Arlosoroff, who at the time headed the political department of the Jewish Agency in Palestine.

Salem was always impressing upon the Jewish Agency that the Cochin Jews were ardent supporters of the Zionist ideology and wanted to settle in the land of Israel. Arlosoroff was the leader of the left-wing Zionist Mapai Party, the dominant Palestinian Jewish political force of the time and an advocate of 'strength-based' compromise with the Arab world. On the night of Friday, June 16,

---

9 Salem, *'Palestine to-day'*, The Jewish Tribune, September 1933, pg 51. Cited by Prof Chiriyankandath.

10 King David Hotel is located on King David Street in the centre of Jerusalem, overlooking the Old City and Mount Zion. It is a listed member of the Leading Hotels of The World.

11 Keren Hayesod was set up in London at the World Zionist Congress in 1920 to raise money for the establishment of Israel. Today, it is a registered corporation in Israel with branches in 45 countries.

1933, Arlosoroff was walking with his wife on a beach in Tel Aviv, when he was shot dead by two gunmen. He was only 34 years old. The murder remains unsolved to this day.

Two days later after Salem received the news from Palestine, he sent a telegram to the Mapai Party and the *Palestine Post*:

'I hasten to record our horror at the dastardly crime committed against the Jewish Cause in the Holy Land on the Sabbath night - at Tel Aviv, when our high-charactered, peace-loving, selfless worker Dr. Arlosoroff, fell victim at the hands of cowardly assassins.'

- A. B. Salem, on behalf of the Jews of Malabar, Cochin, India.[12]

•••••

Salem was proud of his Kerala heritage and the fact that one of his ancestors, Joseph Rabban, had been conferred with great honours a thousand years earlier by the Kerala emperor Cheraman Perumal. In his booklet about the Paradesi Synagogue *Eternal Light*, he gives his translation of the inscription in the Tamil-Malayalam dialect. The copper plate grant gives the Jews of Kerala, scores of proprietary rights until the "world, moon and sun exists",[13] elevating their political and social status to that of the nobles and warrior classes of medieval Kerala.

In 1933, Salem presented replicas of the copper plates to Yitzhak Ben-Zvi, who was then Chairman of Jerusalem's newly-established Institute for the Study of Middle Eastern Jewry. The replicas were then handed over to the Bezalel Museum.

In an article in the *Palestine Post*, journalist C. Z. Kloetzel, wrote: "Jerusalem's Bezalel Museum[14] has recently been entrusted with an historic treasure, the like of which up to now has only been seen in the possession of the British Museum. When Dr. Immanuel Olswanger returned the other day from a mission to India on behalf of the Keren Hayessod, he brought with him exact replicas of the two so-called Cochin Copper plates.

"These Jerusalem replicas are a gift from A. B. Salem, a promi-

---

12 *The Palestine Post* - June 20, 1933, pg 3.

13 Salem, A.B. *Eternal Light* . Salem's translation of the grant, pgs 55-56.

14 The Bezalel Musuem in Jerusalem, founded in 1912, became the Israel Museum in 1965, with more than 500,000 artifacts and artworks.

nent Cochin Jew to Mr. Yitzak Ben-Zvi[15], in his capacity as Chairman of the newly-founded Institute for the Study of Middle Eastern Jewry... It may serve as a reminder that Jewish science owes a debt to this small remnant of our people."[16]

Yitzhak Ben-Zvi, whom Salem considered a close friend, was a prominent historian and a Labour Zionist leader. He went on to become the second and the longest-serving President of Israel, from 1952 to 1963.

•••••

In the 1930s, Salem was fully committed to the Indian nationalist cause - but he also wrote in his diary that the independence of India from British rule was the 'key to the solution of the Jewish State in the Holy Land.'[17]

In this regard, he was in disagreement with Gandhi and Nehru who viewed Zionism through the prism of imperialism. In fact, Gandhi's opinion on the idea of Israel was: "Palestine belongs to the Arabs in the same sense that England belongs to the English or France to the French ..."[18]

Nehru also told Jewish emissaries like Dr. Immanuel Olsewanger visiting India that he believed Zionism was a movement of high finance and "...We have sympathy for the National movement of Arabs in Palestine because it is directed against British imperialism... Our sympathies cannot be weakened by the fact that the National Movement coincides with Hitler's interests"[19]

Salem's view was: "The love of the Jews for his natural, spiritual home in Zion has never diminished in intensity...may [those] that incessantly work for the cause of Freedom, Goodwill and Peace

---

15 This later became the Institute for the Study of Oriental Jewish Communities in the Middle East, and was renamed in his honour as the Ben-Zvi Institute (Yad Ben-Zvi) in his honor.

16 Kloetzel, C. Z. The Cochin Copper Plates, *The Palestine Post* - July 04, 1950, pg 5.

17 Cited by Cited by Chiryankandath JLMM, *A. B. Salem's diary for 1930-1*, entry for 4 September 1930.

18 *Harijan*, November 26, 1938. Cited by Sreekala S. *Israel's policy of absorption of immigrants": a case study of the Indian Jews.* Dissertation, JNU 2000, pg 83.

19 Immanuel Olsevanger 's *Day by Day Diary in India,* September 22, 1936, Central Zionist Archives (Jerusalem), File: S 25/358 Cited by Sreekala. S. Ibid., pg 85.

on Earth...become partakers in thought, word or deed in the re-gathering of the Wandering Soul of Israel into the Land of their Fathers, in the Mount of Zion...Seek ye the Peace of Jerusalem and Prosper and be Blessed in Peace."[20]

He also exhorted the Jews of India to 'go forth and have a stake in the land of their fathers'.[21]

•••••

Unlike Europe from where Jews flooded into the Land Of Prom-ise because of crude anti-Semitism and violence, the Jews of India were motivated by deep religiosity and desire to live in a place where Judaism is a way of life. Scholars have also opined that Co-chin Jews, the majority of whom were economically deprived, saw this as a way to escape the poverty and immerse themselves in building their own and the future of Zion.

As Rabinowitz wrote: "...the determination on the part of Co-chin Jewry... Malabar Jewry to return to Israel amounts to a pas-sion of Messianic fervour..."[22]

The zeal to reach Israel/Palestine at any cost was sparked into a blaze as early as 1944 when a young Royal Air Force officer named Eliyahu Meir, stationed during the Second World War at Banga-lore, arrived in Cochin. One of the early Cochini immigrants in Is-rael, renowned horticulturist Bezalel Eliyahu,[23] told us during an interview at his farmhouse in Moshav Shahar: "This young man visited the congregations of Chennamangalam, Mala and Paravur, announcing that '...very soon we will all be in a land called Israel.' Our elders called him mad."

While a few stragglers were said to have landed in Israel in 1948, "... it was in December 1948, under the aegis of the Jewish Agency and with Eliyahu Meir as the Group Leader, that the first organized group of 17 Jewish families from Chennamangalam, two from Mala and two from Ernakulam left for Israel. The group of

20 Salem, *Eternal Light*, pg 58.

21 'The time is near', The Jewish Tribune, September 1933, p. 28. Cited by Professor Chiriyinkandath.

22 Rabinowitz, *Far East Mission*, pg 149.

23 Winner of Israel's top Kaplan Award and the Indian Government's Pravasi Sam-man Award (the highest civilian award for people of of Indian origin living abroad).

about 100 people landed in the Fatherland on January 5, 1950...”[24]

The coordinator for the group was one Kadavil Meyer from Chennamangalam.

Bezalel's wife Batzion arrived in Israel in 1954 as part of the Youth Aliyah. "Batzion finished the eighth standard in Cochin and came here. They put her in an institute/boarding school for three years, after which she went to work in Kibbutz Givat Haim.”

Although the policy of the Jewish Agency was to bear the costs of Jewish immigration from all across the world, this was not followed with respect to the Cochin Jews.

Early on, Jewish Agency officials learned of the immense wealth owned by the synagogues of Cochin and that the community was willing to use this to finance their travel to the Holy Land. Soon after the birth of Israel, several Cochin Jews began moving to Bombay to meet officials of the Jewish Agency. They set up a Cochin Aliyah Fund in 1948 with proceeds from the sale of their personal and communal properties.

The same month, Dr. Immanuel Olswanger[25] visited Cochin as an emissary of Keren Hayesod Cochin and met with congregations of all the seven synagogues, exhorting all Jews to make the journey to Israel.

In August 1949, the South Indian Jewish Association had passed a resolution to affiliate themselves with the World Jewish Congress, based in New York, and which was working to help Jews emigrate to Israel. The announcement was made by Dr. I. Schwarzbart, who headed the organization department of the WJC. The announcement also mentioned that the town of Paravur (on the Cochin-Travancore border) had public schools where Jewish children were receiving instruction in Hebrew.[26]

---

24 Eliyahu has also narrated this story to researcher Ophira Gamliel. Gamliel, Ophira, Fading Memories and Linguistics Fossils in the Religiolect of the Kerala Jews, *Oral History Meets Linguistics*, edited by Erich Kasten, Katja Roller,and Joshua Wilbur 2017, 83–105. Fürstenberg/Havel: Kulturstiftung Sibirien. pgs 96-97.

25 Dr. Immanul Olswanger was a folklorist , translator, journalist and Zionist activist. He travelled through Asia in the 1930s and spent a lot of time in India, before settling down in Palestine in 1933. He was said to be particularly fond of the Cochin Jews.

26 *The Jewish Daily Bulletin*, Jewish Telegraphic Agency, August 24, 1949. (Dr. I. Schwarzbart died in New York in 1961.)

In December 1950, Hersh Cynowicz, a Lithuanian Jew who lived in Bombay, reported to the Jewish Agency that the passage to Israel was the driving sentiment of the Cochin Jews. He visited the congregations of Mattancherry, Ernakulam, Mala, Paravur and Chennamangalam where crowds gathered to hear him speak about the establishment of Israel and life in the Jewish state.[27]

(Hersh Cynowicz was instrumental in bringing many of the Jewish congregations of India into the fold of the Central Jewish Board of India - boosting the Aliyah effort. Chennamangalam was the seat of the Malabari Zionist Association).

An emissary named Aryeh Levi from a *kibbutzim* in Galilee visited Cochin in the early 1950s seeking settlers and many of the Jews met him at the residence of Paradesi leader S. S. Koder, including Ruby Daniel who took up the offer (although she had to wait for three months in Bombay to get a flight to Israel).[28]

In March 1951, the Jewish Agency announced that plans for the transfer of the entire Cochin Jewish community by chartered ships were being finalized and it would be done by July of that year after the completion of the massive Iraqi airlift of over 100,000 Jews.[29]

The plan did not materialize because of several factors, one of them being medical concerns about the Cochinis. Emissaries reported that most of them exhibited overt symptoms of filariasis, a mosquito-borne disease.

Officials suggested it could be contagious and most of the Cochinis would become a welfare burden for the country.

Two hundred years earlier, a visitor to Cochin had written about this problem. "The water of this country, near the seacoast - from Cranganore to St. Andreas, which is about 12 leagues, has a bad quality of making the constant drinkers of it to have swelled legs. Some it affects in one leg and some in both. I have seen legs above a yard about at the ankle, it causes no pain, but itching, nor does the thick leg seem heavier than the small one to those who have them; the Dutch used to bring water by boats from Verapoli - but I have seen both Dutch men and women trouble with the

---

27 *Jewish Daily Bulletin*, December 6, 1950.

28 Daniel & Johnson, *Ruby of Cochin*, pgs 96 & 100.

29 *Jewish Daily Bulletin*, March 8, 1951.

malady. And no cure has yet been found to heal it."[30]

And again, in 1834, James Forbes noted in his *Oriental Memoirs*: "...the water of Cochin is unwholesome. Drinking it frequently causes that disagreeable disorder called the Cochin Leg... considered a species of leprosy... I have seen many with a leg thicker than their body...on the naked limbs of the natives it has a disgusting appearance... to the leg of a European with a silk stocking, shoe and buckle something ludicrous..."[31]

In the Cochin Kingdom, the first Western-style medical treatment was introduced by Rev. J. Dawson, a missionary who opened a clinic in Mattancherry in 1818.[32] Other Western-style medical facilities opened soon after, with the first government hospital opened by Diwan Sankara Variyar in 1848 in Ernakulam.

Others were opened at Thrissur, Chittoor, Irinjalakkuda, Thrippunithura, Kunnamkulam, Mattancherry, Vadakkancherry, Kodungaloor, Nelliyampathy, Chalakkudy, and other parts of the kingdom. Filariasis, however, continued to ravage inhabitants near water sources.

A report by a Dr. A. Sternberg, who spent 19 days with the Cochin Jews in 1952, was dismal: 'There is no doubt that 100% of the Jews in Ernakulam are stricken with filaria and some of them will develop elephantiasis - in a most aggravated form in the forelegs, testicles and hands and in some cases on all these parts of the body... Infant mortality is high and babies suffer from skin diseases, eye diseases... 3% to 4% of people tested have tuberculosis... many are not older than 40 and will not be able to do physical work and will soon appear on the list of social workers, since there is no hope of rehabilitation for them...'[33]

Dr. Sternberg was, however, sympathetic. He wrote that the

30 Hamilton, Captain Alexander. *A New Account of the Indies*, London, C. Hitch and A. Millar, MDCCXLIV (1744).

31 Forbes, James and Montalembert, Eliza Rosée. *Oriental Memoirs*, Richard Bentley, London, 1834, pgs 207-208.

32 J. Dawson belonged to the Church Mission Society of England. He also opened the first English school in Cochin - in Mattancherry in 198, which was, however, closed in 1821.

33 Sternberg, Dr. A. *Report on the Cochin Jews,* (MALBEN) Institution for the Care of Handicapped Immigrants, Tel Aviv, 1952, pg 6.

hysteria that got hold of the Cochin Jews was because of the envoys of the Aliyah Department, who approached the Cochini immigration as only a transportation problem and promised a mass *aliyah* without any conditions... without any attempt to know them from economical, social, cultural and health aspects...[34] He then recommended selective *aliyah* on a small scale for the Cochin Jews, not more than 250 or 300 a year.

Reaction to Dr. Sternberg's visit was harsh. "Older generations of Cochin Jews still recall with intense pain the humiliations they faced from the doctor who came to examine them in Cochin. An informant said: 'They behave like Nazis. Of course, the main doctor was a German Jew. He asked us to remove our clothes for examinations irrespective of man or woman. For our women, it was a question of honour. But we had to go through all that...'[35]

The Cochinis had been promised a chartered ship - to take batches of 650 people for a big sum of Rs. 650,000. Most members of the Malabari congregations had sold their shops and homes for pittances - mainly because they had borrowed money using their property as collateral - and were in desperate straits.

Rabinowitz noted: 'Already, elements of tragedy loom ahead... there is a feeling of uncertainty in the air, and their buoyant enthusiasm is not shared by outsiders... but they have a quite conviction that they will return to the home of their fathers...'[36]

In addition, 'the Land of Israel as a home, as a new country and the Land of Milk and Honey with new opportunities ...was packaged and brought to the thousands of Indian Jews by emissaries from Israel and the World ORT Union through synagogues, schools and community gatherings of Jews across India, including Cochin'.[37]

The Israeli Ministry of Health did not want to take the respon-

---

34 Ibid, pg 6.

35 Sreekala, S, *Israel's policy of "absorption of immigrants": a case study of the Indian Jews*, Jawaharlal Nehru University, 2000, pg 96.

36 Rabinowitz, *Far East Mission*, pg 150.

37 Chawla, *Being Indian, Being Israeli*, p98. ORT (Obchestvo Remeslenogo Truda, "Association for the Promotion of Skilled Trades") is a Jewish global education network founded in St. Petersburg in 1880. It currently operates from offices in London.

sibility for the Cochini *aliyah* because of a shortage of funds for medical care and because it would take years to develop some sort of immunization program to protect other new settlers.

Of course, in the end, these worries turned out to be unfounded. Many officials also felt there was no urgency because the Cochinis faced no political or other threats in their homes.

Many of the Cochinis travelled to Bombay where they languished, some of them taking up menial employment, some becoming streetside hawkers - waiting for two or three years before they could leave for Israel. Others lived under tarpaulin tents on the beaches of Kerala, selling fish or fruits.

Jewish Agency officials were reported as saying that the sale of synagogue properties did not yield enough funds for transportation costs, although many Cochinis later 'claimed that there was much more money involved and the Agency simply kept it.'[38]

Several hundred Cochini children ranging from the ages of 12 to 16 were, nevertheless, selected by Youth Aliyah and taken to Israel and sent to some of the 69 centres to be educated so that they would later be able to guide their elders when they come to the country. The flights were from Bombay to Bahrain, stopping at Tehran or Cyprus and then onward to Israel.[39]

Israel's Youth Aliyah program had 12,000 children in its care, with 8,000 of them from Asia and Africa 'to help them make a transition to Western society... A group of Cochin children was taught with great patience that washing with soap was not dangerous.'[40]

•••••

The stranded Cochinis and members of their congregations in Cochin then sent a cable to Yitzhak Rafael[41], a member of the Jew-

---

38 Kushner, Gilbert. *Immigrants from India in Israel,* University of Arizona Press, Tucson, Arizona, 1973, pg 23.

39 Chawla, *Being Indian, Being Israeli,* pg 109.

40 *Youths prepared for life in Israel,* New York Times, September 18, 1960. (Youth Aliyah was first set up in Germany in 1933 by Recha Freier, a rabbi's wife, to send Jewish youth to training programs in Palestine.)

41 Yitzhak Rafael was on the Jewish Agency Board from 1948 to 1953 and he was responsible for bringing in more than 685,000 Jews during the period although he was under pressure to put a cap on the figures. Cable is in the Central Zionist Archives in Jerusalem.

ish Agency's board and head of its *aliyah* department, asking for help with the selective immigration policy adopted by the new state.

That did not work, and in anguish, they turned to A. B. Salem and beseeched him to be their emissary *(shaliah)* to plead their case with Israeli leaders. Salem agreed and set off on February 23, 1953, for Bombay, where he was made to wait for three months.

Shlomo Schmidt, the representative of the Jewish Agency, did not view Salem's mission favourably and delayed granting of the visa to Israel. Before coming to Bombay, Schmidt was the agency's representative in Aden. He apparently wanted full control of the Youth Aliyah movement and the Indian Jewish immigration program and did not want any local interlocutors.[42] (In 1950, Schmidt had made a visit to Cochin to meet members of the community to assess their wealth and suitability.)

Salem arrived in Israel in May 1953 and spent the rest of the year in the country, returning to Cochin only in April 1954. He met with President Yitzhak Ben-Zvi and Prime Ministers Moshe Sharett and David Ben-Gurion, using all his persuasive skills to convince them of the need to let the Malabari Jews into the country.

The Jewish Western Bulletin reported in 1953 about the visit by A. B. Salem to the Holy Land. The paper, in a despatch from Jerusalem, said: "The ancient Jewish community of Cochin, numbering some 2,000 persons, is determined to come to Israel, declared Dr. Abraham Salem, a prominent lawyer... and spokesman for his fellow Cochinese."[43] Salem's visit to Jerusalem came after the successful settlement of 300 Cochin Jews in Kfar Hassidim, in the Valley of Jezreel and other villages, the report added.

While speaking with Israeli leaders, 'Salem interwove his arguments with appropriate passages from the Scripture', such as II Samuel 22:28: "And the afflicted people-thou wilt save."[44] All of Salem's grandchildren have copies of the photograph of Salem sit-

---

42 Hodes Joseph. *From India to Israel: Identity, Immigration, and the Struggle for Religious Equality,* McGill-Queen's University Press, Montreal, 2014. pg 102.

43 *Jewish Western Bulletin,* Thursday, May 14, 1953, page 7. The same report also appeared in *The Jewish Criterion* of May 15, 1953, pg 25.

44 Katz & Goldberg, *The Last Jews of Cochin,* pg 273.

ting across the table with Yitzhak Ben-Zvi.[45] A framed copy is also at Salem House in Mattancherry.

In November 1953, the Israeli Minister of Health announced that German-born physician Dr. Rudolf Reitler, who was a specialist in tropical medicine, would be sent to Cochin along with Salem to investigate the issue of filariasis.

One of the heroes of the Israeli *aliyah* Ezra Haddad[46] was also asked by the Jewish Agency to accompany Salem and Dr. Reitler to Cochin. Haddad later wrote: "An eminent bacteriologist, accredited by the Ministry of Health and the Jewish Agency, arrived in Bombay over a month ago (April 1954) to cure elephantiasis and filariasis among the Cochin Jews, These are the two contagious diseases which have hitherto impeded the admission to Israel of a tribe that has been possessed since the War of Independence with a messianic fervour to join their brothers there."[47]

Salem had just returned to Bombay after pleading the case of the Cochinis in Israel and Haddad described how he and A. B. Salem (whom he addressed as the 'resolute Jewish leader Dr. Salem) were welcomed in Cochin. 'One after the other, the venerable leaders of the Ernakulam, Parur, Mala and Chendamangulam congregations greeted me with 'Baruch Haba'...and bestowed on my neck garlands made of heavy smelling jasmine or gold thread elaborately adorned with stars and tassels...'[48]

Dr. Rudolf Reitler's report on the health of the Cochin Jews was submitted to the Ministry of Health in August 1954.

A letter from one William M. Schmidt from the Department of Health to Dr. Bar-Giora of the Jewish Agency reads: 'I feel that the report is a valuable one, carefully carried out and we are very hap-

---

45 In 1948, Ben-Zvi headed the Institute for the Study of Oriental Jewish Communities in the Middle East, later named the Ben-Zvi Institute (Yad Ben-Zvi) in his honor. He was president of Israel from 16 December 1952 – 23 April 1963.

46 Ezra H. Haddad (1900-1972) was the leader of the Iraqi Jews during the mammoth airlift to Israel in 1950-51, which later came to be known as 'Operation Ezra'. Haddad was a member of the Immigration Department of the Jewish Agency for Palestine and visited several countries on behalf of the United Jewish Association. He was a prolific author and linguist, fluent in English, Hebrew, French, German, Turkish and Farsi.

47 Haddad, H. Ezra. *The Canadian Jewish Review*, Montreal/Toronto, June 4, 1954.

48 Ibid.

py to know that because of the careful and thoughtful planning of public health control measures, no significant danger of transmission of a serious disease now seems to exist in Israel.'[49]

The report was published with additional data by Reitler and Yofte in 1955. Clearance was then given for the Malabaris to enter Israel, based on the recommendations, which included the 'grouping together of ethnically homogenous villages in the hilly parts of the country in the Ramleh area and in the dry Negev in the south. Many were absorbed in the modern and well-established older settlements of the country... [the report] concluded that chances of filarial transmission... in Israel are small...'[50]

Although Salem enthusiastically pushed the Malabari Jews to emigrate, 'he warned them that they would be forced to yield to Western norms - but he could never bring himself to leave his beloved Kerala'.[51] For his services to the Malabari Jewish community and helping them migrate, Salem was presented with a ring and gold medal by the community.[52] The mementoes were last reported to be in the hands of his son, the late Raymond Salem.

•••••

The Cochinis were taken in small batches to Israel. A report on January 22, 1954, read: "A group of 48 Indian Jews arrived [in Tel Aviv] last night on a plane chartered by the Jewish Agency.

"It was announced that the first planeload of Cochin Jews will arrive here on February 7 and that a regular ferrying service for Cochin Jewish immigrants will be inaugurated in March, with three planes arriving monthly until all Cochin Jews who desire to come to Israel have been brought here."[53]

Two months later, another despatch said the Jewish Agency had completed plans for transfer of all the 'Black Jews' from Cochin after they were certified medically fit.

49 Letter, August 19, 1954. *Archives of the American Jewish Distribution Committee, Inc.*

50 Yoeli, Meir MD. Hebrew University Jerusalem. *Transactions of the Royal Society of Tropical Medicine and Hygiene.* Vol 51 No 2, March 1957, London. pgs 127-130.

51 Shenoy, T. V. R. *The Jewish Gandhi and Barack Obama*, Rediff, 8 September, 2008.

52 Cited by Prof. Chiriyankandath, JLMM, *A.B Salem's diary for 1954*, entry for 7 December, 1954.

53 *Jewish Daily Bulletin,* January 22, 1954.

"A party of 70 Jews from Cochin has arrived [in Israel]. They were admitted only after prolonged consideration and after an Israeli medical officer had examined them in India and certified them for entry. The Israeli medical authorities feared to admit them because elephantiasis, a dreaded tropical disease, has infected many members of the Cochin Indian community."[54]

•••••

An Israeli researcher Shimon Lev has written about a Cochin Jew who recounted his tale of this 'medical oppression.' A few months after arriving in Israel, he was sent to Hadassah Hospital in Jerusalem. Without explaining any procedure, the doctor guided his hand into a cage full of mosquitoes. It was only withdrawn after that insects had exhausted themselves stinging it. This incident left marks deep in his heart. "When I interviewed him, he explained that 'everything was for Medinat Israel (State of Israel).'[55]

Lev also wrote that the early arrivals were treated shabbily by the Israeli absorption staff. 'At Tel Aviv airport, the "Jews from the jungle" or blacks as they were referred were considered as people without any culture or identity and were sprayed with poisonous DDT.'[56] Most of the Malabari Jews were settled in outlying areas, some in hostile areas on the border and in the desert or the hills. 'Jews from India were dispersed to Nevatim, Sha'har, and Dimona...all these in the arid, infertile southern Negev region and Indian Jews literally built these townships - digging access roads, laying water and sewage pipes and planting the first trees...'[57]

•••••

Ezriel Gotthelf Carlebach (1908–1956), the first editor of Israel's two largest newspapers, Yediot Ahronot, and Ma'ariv, made a three-week visit to India in 1954. He was one of the leading journalists during the time of Jewish settlement in Palestine and founding of the state of Israel. During his India visit, he met with

54 *Jewish Daily Bulletin*, March 9, 1954.

55 Shimon Lev. *From Cochin to Nevatim: A Moshav Settled by Indian Jews*, Eretz Magazine, Autumn 1992, pg 29. Cited by Sreekala S.

56 *From Cochin to Nevatim*, Eretz Magaine, (1992), Cited by Blady, Ken, *Jewish Communities in Exotic Places*, Jason Aronson, Lanham, Maryland, 2000, pg 244.

57 Chawla, Maina Singh, *Being Indian Being Israeli*, pg 47.

Prime Minister Jawaharlal Nehru and other leaders of the state and the Congress Party. After visiting the Cochin Jews, he wrote in his book, *Account of a Voyage* (in Hebrew, published in 1956): "I had to come all the way here to see genuine Zionism." (There is no mention of him meeting A. B. Salem).

An older generation Cochin Jew in Israel remembers Carlebach's visit to his native Chennamangalam. "We received him with elephants and trumpets. It was like a festival. Any visitor from Israel meant a lot to us".[58]

'Flags, festoons and garlands and the entire Jewish population out in violet trousers, white tunics and cap. Carlebach was amazed to be welcomed by the local parish priest, his amazement deepening as the priest points out to him how close the Hindu temple, the church, the synagogue and the Muslim mosque are.'[59]

By 1955, over 75% of the Cochin Jews had left for Israel - until 1962 when the last of those who were denied entry for medical reasons were permitted to travel. In November 1959, an Israeli soccer team participated in a tournament in Cochin. Large numbers from the local Jewish community - still waiting for *aliyah* - celebrated with gusto when the Israeli team won. An Israeli newspaper '*Ma'ariv*' published a lengthy report about a party thrown for the team by the Jews of Cochin and special trophies gifted to each player. Other newspapers like the '*Davar*' and '*Al HaMishmar*' also reported about the event.[60]

By 1961, there were only a few hundred Cochini Jews left who wanted to go to Israel and it was reported that S. Z. Shragai, head of the Jewish Agency's immigration department, told the Zionist General Council that arrangements would be made soon."[61]

The active synagogues were abandoned and one of the oldest among them - the Thekkumbhagam in Mattancherry built in 1489,

---

58 Sreekala S., Ph.D, Theses, Jawaharlal Nehru University, 2000, *Israel's policy of absorption of immigrants: a case study of the Indian jews Chapter III, Immigration of Indian Jews to Israel*, https://shodhganga.inflibnet.ac.in/ • http://hdl.handle.net/10603/15965

59   https://www.facebook.com/cranganor/posts/they-say-it-was-a-little-jewish-girl-singing-hymns-who-greeted-st-thomas-on-his-/1828415167459466/

60 Barmouth Eliyahu, *The Jews of Cochin in Search of Roots,* Jerusalem, 2001, pg 18.

61 *The Jewish Daily Bulletin*, December 29, 1961.

close to the Paradesi Synagogue and just opposite today's Salem House was demolished by the congregation.

'This was because of the attempt by the Paradesis to take over the building and because of the ages-old disputes between the two communities. Later, one of the Paradesis bought the ruins and built a house over it.'[62]

Most of the Paradesi Jews in Mattancherry and the wealthier among the Malabari Jews - many of whom had businesses and landed properties - had decided to stay back - mainly because the Indian government passed laws controlling the outflow of foreign currency/large amounts of money from the sale of assets.

On January 8, 1961, the World Zionist Congress issued an appeal to Jews all over the world to settle in Israel for 'the good of both the country and themselves.'

The Congress made a special mention of 'about 300 Cochin Jews who have traditionally been small traders but most of those have virtually become wards of the state' and asking the Jewish Agency to get them into Israel quickly.[63]

In 1968, S. S. Koder, who was president of the South Indian Jewish Association, said there were only 300 Jews remaining and they did not want to leave everything behind and go to another homeland to start life afresh. One of the reasons that made educated Jews leave for Israel was the difficulty in finding suitable husbands for their daughters, he said. They lived mostly in Jew Town ...and in the nearby coastal areas of Ernakulam, Chennamangalam and Parur...[64]

The situation changed soon after. The land reformation program of the Kerala government, nationalization of assets and other socio-political changes in India meant that Jews had no place in the order of things. Economically, they were on a downslide and individuals members soon began to move to Israel.

Six years later, in 1974, Koder told the *New York Times*: "We are so few, less than 50 people now. Young boys feel there is no future here... Years ago, we had 14 successive births of girls. Now that

62 Barmouth Eliyahu, *The Jews of Cochin,* pg 19.

63 *Worldwide Appeal Issued at Jerusalem Parley,* New York Times, January 9, 1961.

64 *300 Jews Remain In Cochin,* Jerusalem Post, April 9, 1968.

they've grown up, there's no one from the community to marry.'[65]

(Shabdai Samuel Koder passed away in Cochin on March 10, 1974. He was 86. His daughter Queenie Hallegua still lives in Mattancherry; grandson Dr. David Hallegua is a resident of Beverly Hills, CA and granddaughter Fiona lives in New York.)

For many of the younger Jews in Cochin and the second generation Cochini Jews who migrated years ago, Israel became a transit point to leave for opportunities elsewhere, mostly in the United States. Today, there are two 'White Jews' left in Mattancherry and 15 Malabari Jews in Ernakulam and surrounding areas.

•••••

The last Shabbat prayer in Cochin was held in the Paradesi Synagogue in July 1987, after which there was no *minyan* or quorum of local Jews. The handful of Jews had to wait for Jewish tourists to make up the required number. The synagogue is today a tourist attraction and could soon be taken over by the government to be preserved as a national heritage museum.

The synagogues of the Malabari Jews went into disrepair after they were abandoned, except the Kadavumbhagam Synagogue in Ernakulam market, which is being looked after by its caretaker Elias (Babu) Josephai, although there are no congregational prayers. The Thekkumbhagam in Ernakulam, adjacent to the Kadavumbhagam, has been locked and unused for decades.

The synagogue and the Jewish cemetery in Mala were handed over to the village *panchayat* (administration) after the congregation left for Israel. Controversy erupted after part of the cemetery was turned into a football ground by local political leaders. Activists are now in the midst of an ongoing legal and popular campaign to preserve the town's Jewish heritage.

The Chennamangalam and the 17th-century Paravur synagogues were taken over by the Kerala Department of Archaeology, renovated with new Arks and benches and converted into museums to become part of Kerala's ambitious Muziris Heritage

---

65 Weineaub, Bernard - *Jewish Community in India, Depleted by Emigration.* New York Times, September 19, 1974.

Project.[66] The Kadavumbhagam Synagogue in Mattancherry was turned into a warehouse to dry prawns and later used as a cattle shed; parts of it were destroyed in the rains that lashed Kerala in 2019. Efforts are on to renovate the structure.

In Israel, as the years passed and the Cochinis thrived and prospered in the *moshavim*, members of the community in Moshav Nevatim in the Negev desert built a museum - the Cochin Jewish Heritage Centre - and a synagogue which is a copy of the Kadavumbhagam Synagogue in Ernakulam. The Centre provides a glimpse into Cochini history through an audio-visual presentation about the community, its customs, and a display of original household articles, jewellery and costumes.

The interior of the Kadavumbhagam Synagogue from Mattancherry is today part of the World Synagogues display in the Israeli Museum. The ark, known as *hekhals* (*cabinets or armoires storing the Sefer Torahs*), from the same synagogue was installed in the 1950s in a synagogue in Moshav Nehalim, which has a congregation of German Jews. The ark and podium in the Israeli museum display came from the synagogue of Parur (Paravur).

Today, Cochinis are found in the cities of Jerusalem, Tel Aviv, Petah Tikva, Binyamina and Haifa, in Moshav Aviez and Mesilat Zion - which has road names like Rehov Malabar and Rehov Cochin, Moshav Taoz, and Kfar Yuval in the north, Nevatim, Moshav Shahar, Noram, Kvar Oriya, Tiberias, Yasoda Mala, Ramat Eliyahu, Rishon le Zion, Ashdod, Rehovot and Neot Mordechai.

What Louis Rabinowitz said in 1951 has come to pass. "This community...[will] lose its identity and dissolve itself into the melting pot... of Israel. I must confess to an incurable feeling of sadness when I considered this aspect... that these historic communities... should thus abruptly come to an end, destroyed some of the romance of the miracle of Jewish survival..."[67]

---

66 The Muziris Project envisages a chain of 27 museums, spread over the Cochin heritage region displaying maritime trade, the lifestyles of the inhabitants, artifacts etc. It encompasses mosques, synagogues, palaces, rivers, lakes and canals and when completed is expected to turn Muziris into a major destination for cultural tourism, according to chief project consultant Benny Kuriakose. (Personal communication)

67 Rabinowitz, Louis, *Far East Mission*, pg 9.

CHAPTER IX

Salem In 'Jew Town'

"I don't remember A. B. Salem ever talking about the synagogue or its style of functioning to children or others. There was
no division between members of the congregation outside of the
synagogue. Social and cultural events were celebrated together
and there was goodwill all around, especially during the many
festivals. He used to have grand parties at his house during high
holidays and everybody attended." - *Dr. Essie Sassoon.*

Salem owned two houses on Synagogue Lane. One was very
close to the Paradesi Synagogue on the opposite side of the street
and the other was a little to the north.

Salem lived for some time in Fort Cochin too, in an extension of
the quaint Princess Street, which is today also known as Loafer's
Corner. Princess street was one of the earliest streets to be built
in Fort Kochi and still has an old-world charm because of its European style residences. The house was given temporarily to Salem
by S. S. Koder, then warden of the Paradesi Synagogue.[1]

Mandalay Hall,[2] owned by Salem's ideological foe (in synagogue
affairs) Dr. A. I Simon, was also close to the synagogue.

Later, Salem's youngest son Gumliel bought the house opposite

---

1 Antony, Mathew, grandson of A.B. Salem, personal communication, Ernakulam.

2 Mandalay Hall is today a concept hotel with a high-end antique jewellery store.

the now-demolished Thekkumbhagam Synagogue, where Salem lived in his later years. This property is now a boutique hotel named Salem House, owned and operated by the well-known Casino Group of Hotels, headed by Jose Dominic.

In 1929, Salem wrote the *Eternal Light* - a slim volume about the Paradesi Synagogue that he loved so much although its unfair rules had seriously wounded his soul. Salem's resume, as published in an updated edition of his book in the early 1960s, reads:

- Advocate and Municipal Chairman of Mattancherry.
- Founder-Member of Legislative Council, Cochin, nominated by the Raja of Cochin in 1925.
- Executive Committee member of the Indian States People's Conference for establishment of responsible government.
- Delegate to Indian National Congress session at Lahore (1929).
- First recognized Labour Leader of Cochin.
- Co-founder of Cochin Electric Company.
- Co-founder of Cochin Ferry Services.
- Vice-president of Malabar Jewish Association (1932-47).
- Founder of Indo-Palestine Company.
- Travelled to Palestine and Israel as representative of the Cochin Jewish Community to fight for *Aliyah*.
- Secretary, Cochin Zionist Association.
- Chairman, Board of Trustees, United Synagogues of Malabar (1951-54).

•••••

Although secular in outlook, Salem was deeply religious, who prayed regularly and always wore the *kippah* or the Jewish skull cap. In his book, he wrote: '[Visitors] will see here in Cochin, in this little corner in the extreme south-west of India, the life of the Bible. The same Ancient life continues in the Street, linking the remote past with the present...This little town is not a town at all. It is a Street that has been built religiously and not as a Ghetto, and in it, the Jews of various grades live, clinging to their ancient ideas.'[3]

---

3 Salem, A. B. *Eternal Light or Cochin Jew Town Synagogue*, S.D. Printing Works, 1929 Ernakulam, India. Preface, pg 9.

"Salem was a frequent traveller to Madras by train and a popular story in Jew Town was about one such journey. He was travelling on one of the overnight trains which had sleeping berths. When he woke up, he wanted to pray and began wearing the *teffilin*.[4] His co-passengers thought he was doing some sort of witchcraft or black magic so they forced him out of the train at the next station. He protested loudly but several of the passengers and the travelling ticket examiner were adamant about ejecting him.

"We all heard later that the train had a minor accident before it reached its next scheduled stop. We don't know if this story is apocryphal but Salem did get to Madras by another train long before the train he was forced to disembark reached the station."
- *Dr. Essie Sassoon.*

There was another story about a journey that Salem narrated to Jew Town residents. On a trip to Madras, he got into convivial and animated discussion about politics and government with a fellow passenger. For hours, they agreed and disagreed on many subjects. When they reached Madras Central station, the passenger shook Salem's hand and asked him his name. Salem replied: 'A. B. Salem...; and the passenger, after a pause, shot back: 'If your name is A. B. Salem, I am C. D. Coimbatore.'

(Salem is a city in Tamil Nadu and the passenger thought A. B. Salem was not revealing his name. So he added the name of his city too...Coimbatore, one of the industrial towns in the state.) And they both laughed and laughed...

•••••

Salem kept abreast of news from around the world and wanted to inform his people as well, along with his views on a range of subjects.

He put up a large blackboard outside his home and called it *'The Looking Glass'* on which he pinned newspaper clippings - climbing a small ladder - and wrote his comments on it with chalk, inviting those who passed by to read and discuss issues.

'A. B. Salem educated his own community about Indian Congress affairs, was against reserved seats for minorities, and...drew

4 *Tefillin* or phylacteries (amulets) are cubic black leather boxes with leather straps that observant Jewish men wear on their head and their arm while performing weekday morning prayers.

the attention of Cochin Jews to matters of all India interest. [How-ever] There is no record of his having met Gandhi.' [5]

Salem was aware of what was happening in Germany after the rise of the Nazis in the early 1930s and disseminated news coming out from Europe as well.

He also reportedly alerted his congregation about the German cruiser Emden[6], which called at Cochin in June 1935. A report that appeared in the *Jewish Daily Bulletin* of June 23, 1935, was headlined *'Indian Temple Bars Visit of Reich Sailors'*. It said how the crew of the Emden were not 'permitted by the Jewish Community of Cochin to visit the synagogue of the White Jews, which is a famous show-place for tourists. The Cochin Synagogue is the oldest in India..."[7]

At around the same time, S. S. Koder, who was the leader of the Paradesi Jewish congregation and also a member of the Cochin Legislative Council when the Second World War began is said to have asked Diwan Shanmukham Chetty to allow 250 Jewish fami-lies fleeing persecution in Europe to settle in Cochin.[8] There was no follow-up report about what happened to the request but it is believed that Chetty rejected the proposal despite Koder's and Salem's closeness with the Diwan.

In May 1931, Salem and leaders of the Paradesi community welcomed Jawaharlal Nehru, his wife Kamala and daughter Indira Gandhi when they visited Jew Town.

Nehru wrote in his autobiography, in a chapter titled 'A South-ern Holiday' - "In Cochin, we visited the quarter of the 'White Jews', as they are called, and saw one of the services in their old tabernacle. The little community is very ancient and very unique. It is dwindling in numbers. The part of Cochin, we were told, re-sembled ancient Jerusalem. It certainly had an ancient look about

---

5 Chatterjee, Margaret. *Gandhi and his Jewish Friends*, Springer, New York, 1992. pg 113.

6 The Emden was a light training cruiser of the German Navy. She conducted several training runs in the Indian Ocean region before taking part in naval battles in the Euro-pean theatre and was destroyed in the war.

7 *The Jewish Daily Bulletin*, June 23, 1935, Jewish Telegraphic Agency https://www.jta.org/

8 *Jewish Advocate*, May 10, 1939. Cited by Shalva, Weil, Dr., *From Persecution to Freedom* - essay in *Jewish Exile in India*, Manohar Publishers, New Delhi, 2005, pg 76.

it."[9] Several years later, a picture of Nehru speaking with Salem - after the former had become the Prime Minister of India, was splashed on the front pages of several newspapers.[10]

Among all the photographs at the Nehru Museum at Teen Murti House in New Delhi, Salem is the only person from Kerala who has a picture alone with Nehru on display.[11]

•••

Notwithstanding his demand for representative government and more power to the Cochin Council members, Salem was a loyal subject of the Cochin Royal Family. He expressed his sentiments in his book thus: "The Jews of Cochin are most loyal citizens and on every Shabbat and Festive Day offer special prayers to bless, preserve, guard, assist and exalt the Raja of Cochin and His Royal Family.... in spite of their tenacious, age-long fond longing to return to Jerusalem.[12] And again: "The Jews even now form a conspicuously marked small live unit of the Cochin State and have been generously accorded a seat in the Cochin Legislature, now occupied by the Author of this work."[13]

American psychiatrist, collector of South Asian art, and historian-researcher, Dr. Kenneth X. Robbins says: "Kerala has been hospitable to Jews and Judaism for over 2,000 years, and Jews have been accepted as Jews, not just as individuals to be assimilated and lost to the Jewish people. They were allowed to be fully Indian and fully Jewish. The relationship between most rulers in Kerala and the Jews was marked by unique and positive interactions and even favoritism. This was particularly true for the relationship with the Maharajas of Cochin."[14]

---

9 *Jawaharlal Nehru, An Autobiography*, London: The Bodley Head, 1942, p. 273; Salem also recorded it in his diary for 1930–1, entry for 28 May 1931 as cited by Chiriyankandath.

10 Clipping with Mathew Antony, Ernakulam.

11 Cited by Katz & Goldberg, *The Last Jews of Cochin*, pg 261. From Shirley Isenburg's *Indian Nationalism and India's Jews*.

12 Salem, A.B. *Eternal Light or Cochin Jew Town Synagogue*, pg 57.

13 Ibid, pg 58.

14 Opening lecture at *'Cochin Diary'* exhibition at the American Sephardi Federation in Manhattan, April, 2006. (Report in *www.jewishindependent.ca/* April 14, 2006).

In 1949, Salem and other senior members of the community welcomed the last ruler of the Cochin Kingdom, Maharaja Rama Varma XVIII, to events in the Paradesi Synagogue marking 2,000 years of Jewish settlement in Cochin. The event was immortalized in one of the many paintings unveiled in 1968 and is now on show in a small gallery in the synagogue. (The princely states of Travancore and Cochin merged in 1949 into one state and in 1956 - with the addition of Malabar Province - became the modern state of Kerala within the Indian Union.)

•••••

Despite being at loggerheads on synagogue affairs with S. S. Koder, Salem joined hands with him to launch several business and other ventures. These included an ambitious plan to bring piped fresh water from the River Periyar in Alwaye and electric power to Mattancherry.

Salem was the Legal Advisor and Secretary of the new Cochin Electric Company - with Koder as the Managing Director, and it was Salem who was called upon to negotiate with Parukutty Nethyar Amma, the Consort of Maharajah Rama Varma XVI (1914–1932), who was the power behind the throne, to develop plans for the electricity company and The Cochin Ferry and Transport Services in Kochi - both of which became incredibly successful businesses. The ferry service linked Cochin with Ernakulam across the bay and several of the small islands.

As the years passed, however, Salem and Koder bickered over company management and "in 1944, Salem lost a case for wrongful dismissal as the legal adviser to the electric company, while in the following year he won another case maintaining his claim to shares in the Ferry and Transport Services, which the Koders held that he had forfeited".[15]

"They (the Koders) became very rich, we didn't," said Gumliel Salem. "Also, my father did not have the inclination or the ability to chase after big money."[16]

The business quarrels did not affect their social relationships.

---

15 Cited by Prof. Chiryankandath, James. *The Cochin Law Reports*, vol. 36, 1944/5, pp. 238–42, 557–83.

16 Gumliel Salem, Personal Communication.

Both the Salem and Koder families got together for social and cultural events and their children and grandchildren studied and played together and were the best of friends.

•••••

Although a master of the English language, Salem had a quirky sense of how the language should actually look like in print and in 1912 he became a member of the 'Simplified Speling Sosieti' of 44 Great Russell Street, London, along with Prince Rama Varma of Cochin who then lived in Thrippunithura Palace.[17]

Such was the interest generated by the society in India (because George Bernard Shaw was also a member) that several prominent people joined it in the founding year. These included: P. T. Srinavasa Aiyangar (Madras), an Indian historian, linguist and educationist who wrote books on the history of South India; G. V. Appa Row (Ootacamund), noted Telugu writer; K. S. Desikan (Madras), Eeditor of the Madras Law Journal; L. C. Hodgson (Travancore); W. B. Hunter (Madras), Chairman of the Bank of Madras; S. E. Ranganadham (Madras); C. S. Rangaswami (Madras), secretary to the Maharaja of Dharbhanga and owner-editor of Indian Finance of Calcutta; R. Sadagopachari (Madras); Subramani Aiyar (Malabar); P. G. Sundavera Sastri (Trichinopoly); Suryanarayana, B. Rao (Madras); and J. A. Yates (Madras).

The society publication said: "THE PIONEER iz publisht everi munth, ecsept for tu munths in the sumer. THE PIONEER iz sent graitis tu aul Memberz ov the Simplified Speling Sosieti.

The anyual subscripshon for Asoesiait Memberz iz a minimum ov wun shiling, that for Ful Memberz a minimum ov fiev shilingz. Mor muni meenz mor pouer tu cari on the campain. Memberz ar urjd tu aplie for leeflets seting forth the aimz ov the Sosieti. Theez and aul uther informaishon wil be gladli sent bi the Secretari ov the Simplified Speling Sosieti.

Of course, the movement did not take off.

Some 30 issues of *The Pioneer* were published. In the United States, Congress intervened and halted a government program to use such 'speling', although it had the support of men like Andrew

---

17 *The Pioneer ov Simplified Speling*, Vol. 1,No5, September 1912. 45 Ladbroke Grove, London. Extracted from: https://archive.org/stream/n05pioneerovsimp01simpuoft/n05pioneerovsimp01simpuoft_djvu.txt

Carnegie and major media houses like *The Chicago Tribune*.[18]
•••••

South African Rabbi Louis Rabinowitz described A. B. Salem as "a remarkable man... an intelligent, cultured and learned Meshuchrar... whom I did not have the pleasure to meet." All his information came from his host S. S. Koder.

Rabinowitz did visit Salem's house and interacted with his eldest son Raymond Salem, to look at various documents including a rare bill of manumission for a servant woman named Hannah "dated This day, the 11th of Nisan - on the eve of Passover the Festival of Freedom, in 1886," and said that her sons would be counted in the minyan or the quorum for synagogue prayers. Raymond, of course, rejected his pleas to give him the document for preservation abroad. Rabinowitz also tells the "story about a nasty frame-up" to besmirch the name of Salem after his second son Balfour married Seema Koder (in 1950) and left Cochin as part of his work with the federal Government. (Balfour was an engineer with All India Radio. See his son Leslie Salem's letter, page 22.)

Some members of the Jew Town elite apparently began questioning the religious legitimacy of Salem and his family. The wretched story as told by Rabinowitz was that Salem was born as a result of an adulterous relationship.

It was also alleged that A. B. Salem's wife Ruth was the daughter of a *meschuchreet* (a female manumitted slave), who left her *meshushrar* husband and converted to Christianity. A rumour was also spread that this former female slave had an adulterous relationship with a local Christian. Ruth was then brought up as a Christian who converted to Judaism only to marry A. B. Salem.

Rabinowitz writes: "Now", said [a senior community leader] to me, "the son of A. B. Salem and Ruth has married this white woman, and they have already borne a male child. Is this child legitimate? The paternal grandfather of the child is a *mamzer*, the grandmother a convert, born out of incest."[19]

The Rabbi wrote that he questioned the basis of the story by

---

18 https://publicdomainreview.org/collection/the-pioneer-ov-simplified-speling-vol-1-no-1-1912

19 Rabinowitz, *Far East Mission*, pgs 119-120.

asking pertinent questions about why these issues were not raised when the marriage took place or at the time of A. B. Salem's birth itself. He wrote that at a congregational meeting, he (Rabinowitz) then made a ruling to the White Jews who listened "in deathly silence" that the marriages and the births were all legitimate and unblemished according to Jewish law. [20]

Gumliel Salem said nothing of that sort had happened within the congregation. "There was no sleazy talk of any kind during Balfour's wedding despite the opposition to the relationship. I think the Rabbi was just trying to project himself in his book as a respectable and responsible mediator and one who could solve outstanding issues here in Cochin. He was only here for a couple of days and suddenly became a scholar of our entire 2,000-year history... I don't remember hearing of any such incident."[21]

A 1757 entry in the Paradesi records book stipulated: "If an Israelite or Ger [convert] marries a woman from the daughters of the Black Jews [Malabaris] or the daughters of the Mschuchrarim, the sons who are born to them go after the mother; but the man, the Israelite or Ger, he stands in the congregation of our community and he has no blemish [pagam] [22]

•••••

Salem was a prolific diarist, jotting down his activities and observations on many subjects. These diaries, which he started writing in 1913 continued until 1959, until he suffered a stroke.

Unfortunately, after his death, his eldest son Raymond Salem

---

20 "In Cochin, definitions of Jewish "substance" or "blood" went several steps further. Not only were the Cochinites concerned about a mother's substance, but the purity of a father's substance as well. Marriage and sexual relations were, there fore, of paramount concern, because if the Jewish blood of a couple was considered "tainted," the partners and offspring of that union were no longer recognized as "proper" Jews by the Cochin community."
- Barbara C. Johnson, *Our Community' in Two Worlds: The Cochin Paradesi Jews in India and Israel* (Unpublished Ph.D. dissertation, University of Massachusetts, 1985), pp. 109-110., Cited by Katz and Goldberg, The Sephardi Diaspora in Cochin, *Jewish Political Studies Review 5:3-4 (Fall 1993)*. pg 106

21 Personal communication, Mattancherry.

22 Cited by Katz and Goldberg, The Sephardi Diaspora in Cochin, *Jewish Political Studies Review 5:3-4 (Fall 1993)*, pg 120.

was persuaded to hand over 24 volumes of these diaries relating to the Cochin *Aliyah* and other valuable historical anecdotes to a Rabbi Bernard Kimmel (1922-1991) who was travelling around the world, scouring for Judaica to be deposited/exhibited at the Magnes Museum in Berkeley, California.

The Magnes Museum in Berkeley says on its website that in 1967 (the year that Salem died in Cochin), Rabbi Bernard Kimmel and Yosef Miller conducted Magnes Museum 'rescue missions' for objects of Jewish culture in India and Iran.

Magnes also says that 'Jews fled their communities in and around India and...material culture was being actively destroyed, artifacts from these communities were at risk of vanishing altogether...Rabbi Bernard Kimmel, travelled to these areas, sometimes at great personal risk...'

No Jew has ever faced personal risk in India! The Cochin Jews have told this writer that no Jew or Rabbi Kimmel himself faced any problems in Cochin in the late 1960s. Many of the Paradesis remember the Rabbi as having visited several homes on Synagogue Lane to ask for donations of documents and Jewish religious objects.

Some, however, said it was better that the collection went to the museum, instead of them being sold and peddled at scrap dealers in and around Fort Kochi and Mattancherry (where school textbooks and notebooks with names of Cochini Jews on the fly leaf can be found even today by diligent hunters.)

(This writer could find little information on Rabbi Bernard Kimmel. An obituary notice in the southeastern Connecticut newspaper The Day on Tuesday, Dec. 31, 1991, said Rabbi Bernard W. Kimmel, of San Gabriel, California, had died on Dec. 25 at Huntington Memorial Hosptial in Pasadena. It could not be verified if this was the same Rabbi Kimmel.)

The transfer of these diaries and other national treasures from India to several foreign organizations resulted in Indian historians/researchers being unable to access/get information about a crucial phase of Indian history, without incurring great expense.

The diaries are listed as CASE A - A. B. Salem papers (1913-1959) - Gift of Raymond and Balfour Salem, Bernard Kimmel collection, 1967.0.15 in the Warren Hellman Gallery of the Magnes Museum.

Salem's third son, Gumliel, however, said that his brother Balfour or others in the Salem family - except Raymond - had no role in the 'gifting' of these documents.

Magnes has, however, done a creditable job with its Cochin Jewish collection. From September 10 to December 13, 2013, it mounted an excellent exhibition of over 100 items, including documents and ritual Jewish arts and crafts, curated by Francesco Spagnolo, and with Dr. Barbara Johnson as a visiting scholar- titled *Global India: Kerala, Israel, Berkeley*, presented by Bancroft Library, University of California, Berkeley, Warren Hellman Gallery and Charles Michael Gallery.

The Salem papers of The Magnes Collection of Jewish Art and Life comprise *(as listed in the 2013 Berkeley Exhibition Catalog) are:*

1. 1933 (Diary No. 5): February, 1933: Travels in Palestine (Bethlehem and Hebron).

2. 1947 (Diary No. 6): September 11, 1937: Visit to Kochi by American anthropologist David G. Mandelbaum.

3. Political Pamphlet "No. 1. A Scheme for a Constitution in Cochin", written by A. B. Salem, 1924 and printed in Ernakulam.

4. An Express Inland Telegram draft, sent by Salem on July 20, 1950 to one Abramicha of the Thekkumbagam Synagogue in Ernakulam, with a copy to the Caretaker of the adjacent Kadavumbhagam Synagogue. The telegram reads: "Jerusalem Immigration Department considering your *aliyah* arrangements. None should leave Ernakulam till called for."

5. 1926 (Unnumbered Diary)
6. 1930-1931 (Diary No. 3)
7. 1931-1932 (Diary No. 4)
8. 1938-1939 (Diary No.7)
9. 1939-1940 (Diary No. 8)
10. 1941-1942 (Diary No. 9)
11. 1943-1944 (Diary No. 10)

Salem is also seen in several photographs and a film shot in Cochin in 1937 by David Mandelbaum in 1937, part of the items in the Magnes Kerala collection.

•••••

A slide show produced by Helen Sirkin titled *Simchat Torah 1965 in the Paradesi Synagogue* was presented at a lecture in the Mary Pickford Theater of the US Library of Congress in Washington D.C. on October 11, 2007. Sponsored jointly by the Library's Asian Division, Asian Division Friends Society, B'nai B'rith Klutznick National Jewish Museum, Embassy of India, Friends of Indian Arts, LCPA Hebrew Language Table and the University of Maryland's Office of International Programs, the display also featured pictures of A.B. Salem.

The picture on the cover of this book was taken by Helen Sirkin during the 1965 Simchat Torah celebration in Mattancherry.

(Helen and her husband Abraham Sirkin had done a survey of Kerala synagogues for the International Survey of Jewish Monuments in 1998. Helen Sirkin was born in Woodstock, Ontario in 1925 and grew up in Greenwich, Conn. Her husband was a US Foreign Service Officer and they spent some years in south India during the 1960s, during which time she visited Mattancherry. She passed away in 2013 at the age of 88.)

Helen Sirkin's daughter Dr. Susannah Sirkin of Boston, Massachusetts, remembers Salem whom she met in Cochin when she was a child. "I recollect him as an intense man with a long, white beard, animatedly telling stories about his visits to Israel..."[23]

---

23 Personal communication.

CHAPTER X

The Salem Family

In 1915, Salem was a rising young lawyer and began considering marriage. He set his heart on one of his relatives Ruth Paulose.

•••••

Salem's cousin Hannah (daughter of Avo's son Itzhak) converted to Christianity in the late 1800s after marrying a man named Paulose[1]. They had a daughter Ruth (born on May 22, 1887), who completed her medical studies from Madras and became an LMP - a licenced medical practitioner.

Ruth had a flourishing practice as a gynecologist in Mattancherry with her own clinic and all the Jews of the Paradesi congregation went to her with their health problems. She took care of almost all of the childbirths those days in Jew Town. She also worked in the Government hospital at Ernakulam.[2]

Ruth's uncle Japheth (Itzhak's son) went to work with the Baghdadi Jews in Calcutta and later sailed to England where he opened a restaurant. After that venture failed, he returned to to die in Cochin. Salem used his political influence to get the author-

---

1 A derivative from the Biblical name Paul. Kerala Christians use the name Paulose, Paili and Pailo.

2 The Ernakulam General was founded by Maharaja Rama Varma XIII (1844–1851) of Cochin in 1845.

ities to open a closed and forgotten
Jewish Cemetery in Fort Cochin, so that
Itzhak could be buried next to his father
Avo.[3]

Salem was barred from marrying in
the synagogue by the elders of the
Paradesi congregation, citing his bride's
lineage. So he travelled all the way to
distant Calcutta to marry Ruth on
November 17, 1915, in the Baghdadi
Jewish Magen David Synagogue there.[4]
Ruth converted to Judaism at the synagogue.

Ruth Salem

Salem's *ketubbah* or the Jewish marriage contract is now part of
the Magnes Collection in Berkeley. The *ketubbah* names the couple
as Avraham ben Baraq Salem of Cochin and Ruth bat Avraham,
and features 'animal and floral motifs, a sailing ship, and several
symbols based on Jewish scriptural sources... and inscribed with
the blessing "with God's help we will do and succeed"'.[5]

The *ketubbah* listed the Ten Commandments at the top and there
are signatures by the witnesses in Hebrew at the bottom - while
Salem signed his name in English.

•••••

Veteran Kerala journalist Ravi Kuttikad says he had heard of
Dr. Ruth Salem owning an establishment near today's St. Teresa's
College in Ernakulam, off Park Avenue. Her practice was flourishing and it is said she made a lot of money during the Second World
War when her institution was given a contract to manufacture
tincture of iodine. (Tincture of iodine was used as an antiseptic/
disinfectant when dealing with most wartime injuries and also to
purify drinking water in unhealthy locales).[6] This information,

---

3 Daniel & Johnson, *Ruby of Cochin*, pg 18.

4 Cited by Chiriyankandath, James. *Salem Diaries*, (1913-59, Judah L. Magnes Museum,
Berkeley, California The synagogue was built in 1884 by Elias David Ezra in memory of
his father David Joseph Ezra, who was a real estate tycoon in Calcutta.

5 The Magnes Collection, *Global India: Kerala, Israel, Berkeley Case Study No. 4*, December
2013.

6 Personal communication.

however, could not be corroborated as no member of Salem's family or Cochin Jews in Israel remembers Ruth Salem operating such a facility during the war years.

When she grew old and was in failing health, she lived her last years in Ernakulam with daughter Malka and her family. Ruth passed away peacefully in August 11, 1960, and was buried in the Paradesi cemetery.

•••••

Salem and Ruth had five children - three sons and two daughters, who all grew up to be accomplished individuals in their own right despite the lack of much attention from their illustrious father. According to his youngest son Gumliel Salem: "When we were young, he was a great man outside of Jew Town, but he did not have much time for us. We usually had to fend for ourselves - except when he wanted us to accompany him to the synagogue for his protests.

"However, as he grew older and started withdrawing from active political life, he became closer to us. But we had all grown up by then and had our own lives, families..."[7]

Salem named his children keeping in mind both ancient Jewish heritage and modern history.

The eldest son was named Raymond (born on September 21, 1919) from the Germanic Raginmund (meaning protection) or the French Raimund (meaning wise counsel). The name was apt because Raymond obtained a law degree and had an office in the sprawling home which Salem owned near the synagogue.

However, Raymond did not set up a personal practice. He went to work with the Koder group (that had diverse interests and was one of the wealthiest families in Kerala at the time) as their legal advisor on a salary and was mostly based at the Koder offices on Wellington Island, just off Cochin.

After Salem's death, it was Raymond who gave away his diaries and other papers to Rabbi Kimmel - which were deposited at The Magnes Collection Of Jewish Art And Life, University of California, Berkeley. Raymond Salem was a member of the Cochin Synagogue Quater Centennial Committee of 1968, along with community

---

7 Gumliel Salem, personal communication, Mattancherry.

leaders S. S. Koder, J. E. Hallegua and J. E. Cohen.

The celebrations were attended by then Indian Prime Minister Indira Gandhi. The committee produced an informative booklet at the time and the Indian Postal Service also issued a commemorative stamp featuring the synagogue.

A local artist named Krishna was commissioned to create a set of paintings about the Jewish history of Cochin. The paintings - depicting the first arrival of Jews in the Cochin Kingdom over a thousand years ago to the time of the merger of Kerala with the Indian Union after independence - are on exhibit today in an antechamber of the synagogue.

Raymond visited Israel once but returned to Cochin because he was not enamoured with life in the Holy Land. Like his father and his younger brother Gumliel, he wanted to continue living in his beloved street and place of birth.

Raymond did not marry but had a companion in his later years - a Christian woman who was a distant relative from his mother's side. They lived in a huge house - which was bought by his brother Balfour years earlier - on Synagogue Lane. The house was sold to local businessmen after Raymond's death on September 16, 1990. (He was said to be a wonderful host to visiting scholars, including Dr. Nathan Katz and Ellen Goldberg who lived with him for a year while researching the community).

•••••

Salem's second son, born in 1923, was named Ebenezer Balfour in honour of Lord Arthur James Balfour, who was British Foreign Secretary when he issued the famous Balfour Declaration which first talked of a Jewish state.

The Balfour Declaration was a statement issued by the British government in 1917 during the First World War pledging support for the establishment of a "national home for the Jewish people" in Palestine, which was at that time an Ottoman region with a small Jewish population. The declaration read:

His Majesty's government views with favour the establishment in Palestine of a national home for the Jewish people, and will use their best endeavours to facilitate the achievement of this object, it being clearly understood that nothing shall be done which may

*prejudice the civil and religious rights of existing non-Jewish com-
munities in Palestine, or the rights and political status enjoyed by
Jews in any other country."*

The declaration generated support worldwide for the Zionist
philosophy and Salem was fascinated with its implications.

•••••

Balfour got his engineering degree from the prestigious College of Engineering at Guindy in Madras, founded in 1794 and the
oldest technical institution to be established outside Europe. In
1950, he generated a storm that shook up Jew Town. Balfour declared his love for Seema (Baby) Koder, a member of the so-called
high clan. (Both Balfour and Seema were born in the year 1922).
Opposition to the marriage was fierce and although most of the
social inequalities had disappeared in the community, they were
not given permission to marry in the Paradesi Synagogue.

"Marry they will," said a determined Salem and travelled by
train - almost a three-day journey - along with Balfour, Seema
and Raymond to Bombay, where the wedding was solemnized in a
Baghdadi synagogue. Members of the community who had settled
in Bombay also did not welcome the couple. In Jew Town, the elders passed a resolution barring Seema from the synagogue.

Balfour soon left Cochin with his wife and settled in Madras
where he worked as an engineer with All India Radio.

However, during Yom Kippur that year, Seema's parents invited her home and 'her parents and in-laws advised her to stay away
from the synagogue during the religious services... [However] the
next morning Seema braved the congregation and walked into the
synagogue to take her old seat upstairs in the women's section.'[8]

Almost all members of the congregation left the synagogue in
protest after she refused to be cowed down by some elders who
hassled her and waited until the services were over.

The ostracism continued when their son Lesley was born and
the community leaders did not allow the circumcision ceremony
to be held in the synagogue. The family got the ritual done in one
of the Malabari Jewish synagogues in Ernakulam (but the community celebrated the event with a feast at one of the large residenc-

---

8 Katz & Goldberg, *The Last Jews of Cochin*, pg 155.

es - Sassoon Hall - without the Salem family.)[9]

A few years later, the situation changed - when Balfour and Seema settled in Cochin after Balfour's assignments in various parts of India. The family, along with their son Leslie and daughter Cynthia, was embraced as full members of the community. '[And]... when this boy Leslie grew up, he got married to the granddaughter of A. B. Salem's arch enemy Dr. A. I. Simon - (Glennis Simon). At that time, I was wondering what was happening between the grandfathers in their graves!'[10] The entire congregation joined in the wedding celebrations in the Paradesi Synagogue.

(The Jerusalem Post reported on January 11, 1979: "The small Jewish community of Cochin celebrated its first wedding in a decade recently in the 410-year-old synagogue. The bride, Glennis Salem, an Indian army doctor, was married to Leslie Salem, a Cochin Jew who is now doing research in physics at Haifa University."[11])

In Cochin, Balfour teamed up with his brother-in-law Nappy Koder to start production of fiberglass fishing boats under the brand name of Gamma and Kappa. They also started a venture called Polar Ice Factory to make huge ice blocks for the fishing trawler industry. Both businesses later closed down.

After Jew Town began to 'evolve' as a town without Jews, Balfour and Seema moved to Israel to be with their children Leslie and Cynthia and their families. Balfour died in Israel in 1992. Seema passed away in Haifa in 2015 - a life happily spent with her children and grandchildren. Leslie and Glennis have two children, daughter Galia and son Gilad.

Glennis Salem remembers how, as a young girl, she was also fascinated by Salem's story-telling abilities. "I remember him talking to us about Judaism and narrating Biblical stories as all children gathered around him listening raptly. He was a very clever man, very articulate and had this great command of language...

"He used to have a daily 'thali' (a traditional metal meal plate) early in the morning, with small containers of different powders,

9 Ibid, pg 157.

10 Daniel and Johnson, *Ruby of Cochin*, pg 21.

11 Report from *The Jerusalem Post*, as printed in *The Bulletin,* January 11, 1979, Multicultural Canada archives.

which he said were nutritious. One of them was gold dust[12]... (*in Malayalam it is called thangabhasmam.*)"

"I also remember stories of his travel to Israel where he met Levi Eshkol, then Minister of Finance in Israel - and took the Bible with him for a meeting. He also asked Prime Minister David Ben-Gurion: "Where in the Bible is it mentioned that Jews with any ailment cannot live on Jewish land...?"

(Salem's trip in 1953 to Israel was to represent the Malabari Jews and deal with their immigration and related health problems. See Chapter on Salem, Zionism & Aliyah - page 144.)

•••••

Cynthia (Balfour and Seema's daughter) and Muralee Dharan, a Hindu, were students at Trivandrum Medical College when they fell in love and decided on spending life together. After getting her medical degree, Cynthia made *aliyah*, and lived with her parents and brother Lesley's family in Haifa, Israel.

Muralee worked in several countries before travelling to Israel to live in Kibuttz Givat Haim near Hadera in Haifa district where he learned Hebrew.

Muralee and Cynthia had had a civil marriage in Cochin and in Israel, Muralee converted to Judaism after going through a religious course. He married Cynthia again in a ceremony in a *Rabanuth* - not a synagogue - in 1981.

[Rabanuth is a Jewish court of religious law where important decisions are made, with reference to Jewish law. Having a wedding in a synagogue is not very popular in Israel. They usually have a simple function in the religious court or a grand event in a restaurant or banquet hall.]

(My sister Rachel and I escorted Muralee the groom to his wedding in Tel Aviv from my sister Rachel's house in Petat Tikvah. - Dr. Essie Sassoon.)

The Dharans live in Afula in the Jezreel Valley in the Northern District of Israel, where Cynthia works as a General Physician. Muralee, who retired recently, is an acclaimed pathologist and

---

12 Edible gold has a number allotted to it - E175 and it is widely recognized as a food additive, although it has no nutritional value. In parts of India and the Middle East, it is believed that gold has antiinflammatory and other medicinal properties. The Federation of Synagogues recognizes gold as a kosher *parve* food additive.

has worked in several African countries. The Dharans have three sons - Nadiv (who is married), Dever and Raviv - and all three are highly educated. (*The three sons were delivered at the Ashkelon hospital by Dr. Essie Sassoon*).

•••••

A. B. Salem's third son, born in 1927, was named Gumliel - a figure from the Hebrew Bible - belonging to the tribe of Manasseh. It was also the name of a first-century authority on Jewish law.

Like his elder brother, Gumliel was also besotted with a member of the 'white' congregation, Reema Roby (born October 29, 1929), daughter of the ancient and illustrious Roby family's Ezekiel and Simcha Roby. Gumliel and Reema were also not allowed to wed in the Paradesi Synagogue - so they too travelled to Bombay for their marriage, following in Balfour Salem's footsteps.

After his graduation in Cochin, Gumliel travelled with a scholarship to the United States to get his Masters degree in Engineering from Cornell University in New York. He returned to Kerala - although he had the option to stay on in the United States. He said he loved Kerala too much to stay away.

He worked as an engineer with the Kerala government before turning to teach and was Professor of Mechanical Engineering at the renowned Government Engineering College, Thrissur. He then took up the post of Principal of the Government Polytechnic in Kalamassery, Ernakulam, where he worked until his retirement.

Known as Gummy to everybody in Mattancherry, he was a state-level champion bridge player - representing Kerala and winning several tournaments in India. While visiting Israel in 2003, he teamed up with his relative Aharon Twig and won a national championship game in Petah Tiqva. He also played bridge with international great Omar Sharif in Egypt, according to his son Kenny Salem of Toronto.

A popular member of the famous Lotus Club in Kochi, Gumliel also established a name for himself as an accomplished carrom[13] player. (*The Lotus Club was the first non-white-exclusive club in the kingdom. In the early days of its founding, Lotus Club was a venue for many public debates on contemporary social, scientific and political is-*

---

13 A tabletop board game that is popular in South Asia.

From left: Prakash Rao, Leslie Salem, Reema Salem, Venetia (Mino) - standing, Usha Rao, Linda Salem, A. B. Salem, Seema Salem (standing) and Raymond Salem.

sues. *The first club night was held on September 9, 1932, in the presence of Maharaja Rama Varma XVII.)*

Gumliel was not a devout Jew because of his direct experience and participation in his father's 'battles' in the synagogue and he kept away from congregational worship for several years.

It was only in his later years that he began visiting the synagogue regularly "but only to ensure that there was a *minyan* (quorum) to keep the prayers going when there are Jewish tourists."[14]

"We often wondered why Father didn't move to the Thekkumbhagam congregation, where he would have been welcomed and got the respect he deserved.... And also, despite being well-to-do we were not rich although the Cochin Ferry and the Cochin Electric Company were his (Salem's) ideas. He did all the paperwork, but received no shares in the wealth generated by the company..."[15]

Gumliel and Reema had two children, Linda and Kenny Salem (both of whom live in Canada). Although Linda faced no problem in the synagogue and could sit with others upstairs, Kenny's circumcision ceremony was not allowed to be held in the synagogue; it was conducted at the nearby Sassoon Hall. All differences disappeared soon after and Kenny Salem could read his *Hafttarah* (a selection from the Hebrew Bible) in the synagogue and celebrate

14 Personal communication.

15 Personal communication.

his *Bar mitzvah* (coming of age ritual) with the full congregation.

A. B. Salem had passed away by this time.

Reema worked in Cochin's first power company, the Cochin Electrical Company, which was set up at the initiative of Samuel Koder and A. B. Salem. The company was later nationalized and amalgamated with the Kerala State Electric Board. She also worked for some time with the Cochin Ferry Service, also a venture of Koder and Salem.[16] Reema passed away on August 25, 2015, at the age of 86. Gumliel Salem died on February 23, 2016, aged 89, in a private hospital at Panayapilly, near Fort Kochi.

•••••

Mathew Antony is the grandson of Salem's eldest daughter Dr. Malka Lilly Salem (who became Dr. Mary Antony after her marriage).[17] "My parents met when my father, who loved to play soccer, broke his leg during a local game and was admitted to the general hospital where my mother worked," says Mathew.

There was opposition to their union from both families, one a renowned Jewish family and the other an orthodox Syrian Catholic one. 'However, both were independent and had good jobs and they got married in Madras and later moved to Cochin."

Mathew recounts: "Daddypapa (Salem) had already seen Mino Aunty (Malka's younger sister) marrying out of the community and Judaism, and apparently his heart was broken when his other daughter also did the same. Only a few of Mom's friends from Jew Town attended the wedding.

"When they arrived in Trichur, my paternal grandfather refused to let them enter the family home. So they went to Mattancherry where Daddypapa also said they were not welcome.

"It was then that Grandmother Ruth Salem stepped in. She gave the couple her house (gifted to her by A. B. Salem) on Layam

16 The Koder family established the first chain of department stores in Kerala and were agents for a range of high-end international consumer goods. They also owned and operated the Cochin Electric Company as well as the Cochin Ferries (both of which were set up along with A. B. Salem.) The Cochin Royal Family also held a stake in the electric company which supplied power to Mattancherry and Cochin and other areas up to Palluruthy. The Cochin Electric Company operated from the 1940s till the late 1970s. After nationalization, it became part of the Kerala State Electricity Board).

17 Malka means 'Queen'. Although her name was Malka in Jew Town, as a doctor she was known as Dr. Lilly Salem, until her marriage.

Road in Ernakulam - where they stayed for the next 10 years. They moved to their custom-built home in 1955.

Reconciliation with both sides happened after Mathew's sister Rose was born - by that time both Malka (Mary) and Antony had established themselves in Ernakulam, and both sides needed Dr. Mary's services for the children being born over the years.

C. J. Antony (Chettupuzhakaran Mathew Antony) became a well-known figure because he was the Chief Engineer at the Public Works Department and was instrumental in the conceptualization and completion of the iconic Mahatma Gandhi Road in Ernakulam and the stretch of National Highway No 7. Mary gained fame as one of the leading gynecologists in the city. She also worked for a time at the Mattancherry hospital where her mother Ruth had worked earlier.

The couple built one of the most beautiful houses of that era - - which was named 'Rose Garden' after their eldest daughter Rose - in the upscale area of Ernakulam city (where most of the judges and city administrators live). Mathew was five years old at the time. The art deco style mansion, made of laterite and plastered with lime is still as elegant as it was more than 65 years ago. Most of the furniture in the home like the heavy cupboards and desks came from Mattancherry and were made in the 1950s.

After her marriage, Malka's religious outlook had a drastic change. Mathew says: "My mother never talked about Judaism to us. As ardent as she was as a Jewess, she embraced Catholicism with a fierceness that included going to daily mass (even if she had been working during the night), insisting on daily evening family prayers even if we were going to be late for a movie, saying the evening prayers on our way back from Jew Town whenever we visited, etc. We often went as a family to Jew Town during the years that I was at home, especially for the festivals, and my mother would join in the singing...

"She also never talked to us about her early life in Jew Town and the discrimination and other indignities. I heard most of the stories later from Gummy Uncle (A. B. Salem's third son). Of course, by the time I was born these were stories that had come to an end." Mathew's sister Rose was married to the late Dr. Thomas Alexander - who died in 2015. Rose has two children - (1) Teena Reuben who married Reuben Peter and they have one daughter Malka Reuben; and (2) Dr. Tony Thomas who married Dhanya Paul; and they have two children Tia and Taran.

Rose lived in England for about seven years from 1969 onwards. She did her schooling in the resort town of Ooty (now known as Udhagamandalam) in the Nilgiri Hills, and later her pre-university studies in Madras. Today, she lives in a house adjacent to Mathew's home.

Mathew is married to Marie Therese and they have three children: (1) Mary Grace - married to Tony Mayer [two children - Herman Francis and Naia Lily]; (2) Antony Joseph - married to Paulina [one daughter Celine Marie]; and (3) Mathew Abraham (who is single).

Mathew lived in London, England, from 1971 to 1980 and from 1986 onwards worked a few months each year in Switzerland and through his association with that country in many African countries, Kyrgyzstan, Bhutan, Kosovo and Mongolia. He also did some short stints in Iraq and the United States.

Mathew retired from his software entrepreneurship a few years ago and today organizes conducted study tours a couple of times a year for visitors from Switzerland to South India along with his erstwhile business partner from Switzerland.

Mathew Antony remembers his childhood days with A. B. Salem in Jew Town.

"I remember my grandfather as a man who could tell wonderful stories. All the children would sit around him in the evenings and he would tell us to pick one story from the Bible and he would elaborate on it with a lot of flourish and imagery."

"He was 62 years old when I was born - he had retired from active public life and my earliest memory is of me sitting in his lap and playing with his flowing beard and I would gurgle and he would chuckle..."

"I also remember how great a storyteller he was during our festivals, along with other senior community members like Hallen Hallegua and Nappy Koder and Ruby Daniel's father Japheth. All the children used to gather around his feet listening to the Biblical tales. There were few scholars in Jew Town, so grandfather and a couple of others were the people to go to for guidance.

"As I grew up, I heard about his life and how he was a person who influenced social practices and political discourse in the then Kingdom of Cochin, and even after India got its independence.

"Grandfather was the early face of trade unionism in Cochin - he changed the face of the Cochin labour movement and the struggles for working-class rights - and he always found himself at loggerheads with the administration and the Diwan of Cochin."

"I used to take my bicycle to go to Jew Town from Ernakulam where I stayed with my parents... about 13 to 14 km... Tables would be out on the streets in the evening and there would be card games and board games in full swing and refreshments of all kinds... And of course, Daddypapa was the grand patriarch."

There were many non-Jews who were friends of residents who joined in our festivals, After his wife Ruth died in 1964 at Malka Antony's Rose Gardens home, Salem stayed with the Antony family a few times but preferred to be in Jew Town and near his synagogue. Malka Antony passed away at the of 62 in 1978. Her husband Antony lived in the house until his death in 2001.

Mathew Antony said he visits Mattancherry when he has visitors who want to see the Paradesi Synagogue. He, however, keeps in touch with all members of the community who are in Israel and elsewhere.

"I visited Israel in 1999 and stayed for a week in Haifa. Nappy Uncle and Leslie took me around. I was also invited to make up the *minyan* at the border with Lebanon where one of the guards wanted to recite the *Kaddish* (one of the central elements in Jewish liturgy)."

•••••

Venetia Eshter or Mino[18], as she was called at home, was the rebel among Salem siblings and a favourite of A. B. Salem, from whom she acquired a lot of her fighting spirit during her early

---

18 Mino was named after an aristocratic Englishwoman Venetia Stanley who converted to Judaism after her marriage to Edwin Montagu, then Secretary of State for India (1917 and 1922), and Esther, a Jewish heroine who married the legendary Persian king Xerxes (486 and 465 BCE) and saved her people from being slaughtered. The story of Esther is the basis for the festival of Purim.

years. The discrimination in the synagogue and community rubbed off on her and set the mood for her quarrelsome attitude in Jew Town. She was irascible at times and used to argue about not being given proper seating rights in the synagogue. "Why," she used to harangue everyone, "why are we treated differently inside the synagogue?".

(Both Venetia and Malka seldom went to the synagogue after they became teenagers).

After Venetia went to Madras Medical College for her studies - it was literally an escape from the claustrophobic atmosphere of Jew Town - and got involved in mainstream Kerala life, her attitude mellowed considerably. It was during her medical school years that Venetia met Dr. Pejavur Sadanand Rao, converted to Hinduism and became Dr. Sarla Sadanand Rao.

In Jew Town, of course, there was consternation and condemnation following her decision.

Venetia's daughter Dr. Usha Mohan, who lives in Hubli, says: "Daddypapa was very dignified, however. Before she married, my mother received several letters from him about Judaism and other religions and trying to persuade her to not abandon her faith... I kick myself for not keeping those letters..."

In one letter, Salem told Venetia that there would be difficulties for her in later life. 'You are very young... and all these emotions will pass with time. Venetia, remember you cannot be a Brahmin, you have to be born into it.' Salem ended the letter with "...if you are actually going ahead with it, you will have my blessings."

"Earlier in Jew Town, Mercha uncle had wanted to marry her and tried to court her. He was a doctor but didn't have the courage to go against his mother's wishes and marry a so-called 'Brown Jewess'. "He told Venetia: 'Wait till my mother dies.'[19]

Of course, the mother didn't die and Venetia didn't wait around.

---

19 Mercha was the nickname of Dr Meir Roby, a surgeon who worked in hospitals in Alleppy and Cochin. His mother's name was Simha Koder. Dr. Meir emigrated to Israel and worked there for a couple of years before passing away after being diagnosed with cancer of the colon. He is survived by his wife Rachel and three children, daughters Simmy and Florence (who lives in Australia) and son Ezzie. Both Simmy and Ezzie live in Binyamina and Rachel lives with her daughter Simmy and husband Sammy.

"Matilda's[20] father Elroy also wanted to marry her but my mom rejected his proposal. Elroy later married a Baghdadi Jew, named Sara," recollects Dr. Usha Mohan.

Sadanand was a General Physician; he passed out from Madras Medical College and served a short service commission in the Indian Army and was posted in Rangoon (Yangon in modern Myanmar). Later, he worked in Cochin and Ernakulam before settling down in Hubli where the couple had their own hospital. Dr. Sadanand was very successful as an anesthetist while Dr. Sarla gained recognition as a gynecologist.

Dr. Usha Mohan says: "A few years before my father passed away they retired and gave up the hospital. They never actually owned it. It was rented for about 35 years and the rent was a paltry Rs. 100/- but it was a regular hospital with an operating theatre, labour room and fully equipped. I have also operated in there - whenever I came down to Hubli on vacation from Brunei to meet my parents."

"I have heard that my mother was totally transformed by the red dot on her forehead. She also became fascinated with Hindu mythology and delved deep into the various scriptures and epics. But, it was interesting how later on in life, she began observing the traditional fast during Yom Kippur, along with other Hindu observances."

Venetia was a woman who could charm others if she wanted to. Mathew Antony (her nephew) recounts how during one of her surgery exams she had to give an oral test and the examiner asked her to identify some surgical instruments.

"There were two examiners - one internal and another from outside the college; the latter picked up a steel implement and asked her what it was.

"There was no answer. The question was repeated. Again silence. Then she was asked to pick up any instrument and name it. Mino aunty had frozen and couldn't utter a word. However, the internal examiner was very fond of her so he picked up a piece and asked: 'Is this a retractor?'

20 Matilda lives in Petah Tikva with her husband David Davidson in a house evocatively named 'Kerala House.'

"Mino aunty nodded and the examiner said: 'OK, run along...' She passed the exam."

Dr. Usha recounts: "I remember Daddypapa vividly. He was a grand old man! Mom told me a lot of stories about him. One of my sharpest memories of him was when he came to my school in Hubli to see me. I was a student of Std II and was alone at home one day playing with soda water bottles. One of them broke and a sliver of glass cut my cheek. The next day in school, my teacher told me that somebody was waiting in the courtyard to see me. Imagine my delight to see Daddypapa, with his long white beard and warm hugs... he had rushed from Cochin to see me... the kindest person I ever knew. We only realize the worth of our parents and grandparents when we lose them..."

"I remember him at the Shabbat Table, with the whole family milling around. He would say the prayers and then break the bread; wine would be served in white metal tumblers," recollects Dr. Usha.

"When he had become old and had a stroke, he used to call out Dudu Mole (*Dudu, darling daughter*), come and push me to the synagogue and back... All the other children on the street also used to come and run around him and annoy him. He used to wave his stick at them and mumble 'go...go', but he had a mischievous look when he did this... In his old home, he had a wonderful shade at the front made of '*ramacham*'[21] which kept the interior cool and fragrant when there is a gentle breeze and... the house had exquisite 19th century tables and furniture made of solid teak wood...

"He also had a beautiful cupboard in his room stocked with all kinds of fancy soaps, candles and knickknacks... all the grandchildren loved rummaging through it...

"There was a well in the backyard in which some small tortoises always frolicked - we used to bring them up in buckets on pulleys and he used to shout at us 'Be careful, be careful...'

"Jew Town was great fun during our childhood. School vacation time was when all the children gathered and were pampered by

21 '*Ramacham*' or Chrysopogon zizanioides, commonly known as vetiver is a bunch-grass of the family Poaceae, that grows in the hills of the Western Ghats of India. It has now become a major commercial crop for its essential oil that is used world wide in perfumeries and cosmetics.

the family and the entire community.

"My brother and I went to Cochin every year. The street was ours - and everybody was part of a big family. The ground opposite the synagogue was a favourite place to spend time and Raymond Uncle and Balfour Uncle used to chaperon us during our outings.

"There were many girls - Matilda, Linda, Glennis and others - and we used to go to Hotel Sea Lord for special evenings. For New Year, we frequented the Navy Ball in Cochin. (Cochin is the headquarters of the Southern Naval Command - which has a massive reach deep into the Indian Ocean and the Navy Ball held in December is one of the most anticipated events in the social calendar of the city.) We used to attend the gala at Malabar Hotel... There were also outings to the swimming pool."

"Ruth Salem, whom we all called 'Nani', used to visit us sometimes in Hubli and in her later years she was moving spiritually towards Christianity again, especially after any meeting with my aunt Malka Antony in Ernakulam.

"They used to pray at an altar together...

"In our house, she used to pull our legs saying: 'Ours is the only God... [In Hinduism] you have stories of people with ten arms and ten heads who killed Gods... Who can kill gods? Gods cannot be killed. Oh no, don't pray to such Gods...' She used to laugh. But there was no malice in her words and my mother was a devout Hindu." In old age, Ruth suffered from severe depression and her demeanor changed completely. "My father used to say that Nani Ruth was such a talkative person, easygoing with everybody in Jew Town and see the transformation..."

•••••

Dr. Usha or 'Dudu' as everyone in the Cochin Jewish community calls her, married Dr. Mohan Rao and they moved to Brunei where they worked for 15 years - from 1992 to 2008 - before returning to Hubli to continue their practice.

They have two children - daughter Neema and son Nikhil. Neema is married to Kevin Cox (they have three children Kylah, Nikhil and Ashon) and they live in Salisbury in the United Kingdom, but Neema also holds Australian citizenship. Son Nikhil Mohan and his wife Alison have one daughter, Kylah, and they live in Australia, although they hold dual Australian and Canadian citizenship. Dr. Mohan Rao passed away on April 1, 2020, after a battle with cancer.

•••••

Venetia also had a son, Prakash Rao, who disappeared mysteriously about two decades ago. He apparently left home to receive his relative Dr. Leonore Mariam Simon (Glennis Salem's sister) who lives in the US at Bangalore airport. He never reached there. A police hunt was launched all over India but there is no word until today about what happened to Prakash Rao.

Prakash, who was very close to members of the Paradesi congregation, has been described as a brilliant engineer who had a great career and life ahead of him. Many people, however, think that he is still alive and will surface one day.

•••••

Linda Hertzman is the eldest daughter of A. B. Salem's youngest son Gumliel Salem and wife Reema. Linda lives in Vancouver, British Columbia, where she and her husband Steve run a *kosher* food store and a successful catering business called Classic Impressions.

She specializes in gourmet *kosher* cuisine tailored to events ranging from small luncheons to grand weddings. (Linda is the elder sister of Kenny Salem, who lives in Toronto).

Linda has an MA in Psychology from the University of Kerala in Trivandrum and moved to Israel in 1982.

Linda and Steve first met in Mattancherry when Steve, who was born in Toronto, was visiting Kerala as part of a business trip to India. They kept in touch over the next two years and later got married in Israel in 1984. That same year, Steve and Linda moved to Canada, opening a *kosher* store called Raisins, Almonds & More at Bathurst and Sheppard in Toronto.

Linda, meanwhile, also enrolled at the George Brown College cooking school and at Seneca College, taking courses on food service and management. In 1994, they decided that Vancouver would be a better place to settle down and bring up their children and moved to British Columbia, first purchasing a restaurant called Leon's and renaming it as Aviv's Kosher Meats.

About her illustrious grandfather, Linda says: "I remember Daddypapa as a man of somewhat strict demeanour but very soft and loving inside. I remember my parents telling that he was so involved with things outside the home, including high politics of the Cochin kingdom, that he had no time for his family.

"When his grandchildren were growing up, he had stopped most of his political activities and seemed a little disillusioned with the state of affairs in modern Kerala.

"Daddypapa had a wonderful old cupboard which was stacked with books and we brought many of them with us to Vancouver." Many of the books also belonged to A. B. Salem's elder son Raymond.

Salem's collection includes commentaries on Jewish law and writings about the Babylonian captivity. Two of the books show the edition year as 1870 and were printed in Warsaw, Poland, and another as printed in Germany in the early part of the 20th century. There are also some volumes with songs, prayers and opinions by different rabbis on various aspects of Jewish law and includes passages in the Aramaic script.

Linda and Steve have three sons - Nathan, Joshua and Shayne.

•••••

Kenny Salem (the son of Gumliel and Reema Salem) got his Bachelors of Engineering degree from the Regional Engineering College in Thrissur. He left Kochi at the age of 25 in 1987 and lived in Israel for three years where he worked in the Negev, became fluent in Hebrew and well-versed in Sephardic customs and lore before following his sister Linda to Canada in 1990.

Kenny was only four years old when A. B. Salem died in 1967 at the age of 85. He has vivid memories only of his grandfather's funeral.

"All of the children in Jew Town were up on a balcony in a house belonging to Johnny Hallegua, near our home and watching the crowd swell downstairs. I think everybody from Kochi was there. He was such a well-known figure and the funeral procession to the cemetery was a massive one. Alongside his grave are my parents' graves and on the other side is Raymond Uncle's and Grandmother Ruth's graves."

In India, Kenny was active in motorsports, participating in the gruelling Himalayan Rally and other races. Kenny runs a transportation business in Toronto. He lives with his wife Deborah (who is of Polish descent through her mother) and daughter Alexis in King City, north of Toronto. He attends the BINA congregation (Bene Israel of North America) at the Jewish Women's Council premises in Toronto.

Kenny and Deborah married in a convention centre in Thornhill (Vaughan) in 1999. His parents Gumliel and Reema Salem came to Toronto for the wedding. Other guests included members of the Paradesi Community and relatives from Cochin who have settled in Israel and the U.S.

The marriage was conducted in traditional Cochin style with the bridegroom taking the lead in ceremonies. Rabbi Berman from the Shaar Shalom Synagogue near Don Mills and Steeles in Toronto (which was closed and demolished some years ago) was present as a witness and to sign the contract. Rabbis do not have much of a role to play in Cochini weddings.

•••••

Abraham David's grandmother Leah (Lulu) was A. B. Salem's first cousin. Abe remembers the long, white beard sported by Salem. "I also recollect how he used to sit in his wheelchair and all the children used to have fun pushing it to the synagogue and him waving his stick at them."

Abe says his friends were mostly out of Jew Town because he attended St. Albert's School and Maharaja's College - but remembers that Salem had 'put up a notice board outside his house near today's Ethnic Passage store to post political news and comments.'

"Salem Uncle - Bless him - was a very ambitious man. He was very faithful to his countrymen and at the same time religious. Even in 1972, after most of the Cochin Jews had left for Israel, there was still some activity in Jew Town because people used to come to meet members of the Koder family.

"There were not many shops on Synagogue Lane - I remember it as quite bustling with only Jews walking about. Today, when we visit, it is dark and lonely in the evening - there is nobody on the streets, the shops owned mostly by Kashmiris are shuttered and the atmosphere is eerie," says Abe.[22]

Abraham and his wife Lillian Ashkenazy live in Tiberias, where his sister Sippora (Venus) and her husband Herbert Lane also reside. Of his two brothers, Pinhas David and his wife Zipporah live in Petah Tikva, while Morris David and wife Reeni Ashkenazy live in Haifa.

•••••

Dr. Essie Sassoon: "My mother was a widow and we had a tough life in Jew Town. The synagogue helped our family with money and we have always been thankful to the elders of the congregation. A. B. Salem was a religious man and always ready to help those in need. In those days, it was difficult for a single girl to travel long distances alone. He accompanied me to Madras when I wanted to join the Christian Medical College - before I secured admission for my medical studies in Kerala itself - in the University of Calicut.

"Madras was a tough trip. We had to travel first by train to a place called Shornur and then take the steam-engine driven train to Madras - the travel time was about 18 to 20 hours. He was quite used to this. In his early years, Salem had to travel in a small boat to Ernakulam from Mattancherry, before the artificial Wellington Island was made. From there he had to ride in a bullock cart to reach Shornur, and from there to Madras.

"As a child, I always looked up to Salem's daughters Malka and Mino and all the young girls in Mattancherry wanted to become doctors like them and their mother Ruth. It was their drive and success that inspired me also to join the medical profession."

"Salem was very strict about *kosher* food and would eat only vegetarian food when out of Jew Town. He was also very generous, bringing back baskets of mangoes for members of the congregation from wherever he went. He was very fond of showing all of us the different varieties of mangoes he had been able to find."

•••••

Salem was an irascible and fearless personality always speaking his mind, unaware or uncaring of what people around him felt about his actions and words.

Pearly Simon, who now lives in Haifa (Israel) describes one

---

22 Personal communication.

such incident: "Many Jew Town families had flourishing coconut and fruit estates on the island of Vettakka. I have heard of how some of the plantation workers rebelled against the families for not meeting their demands for higher wages. Some of them came to Jew Town with red flags and shouted slogans on a Saturday afternoon. Besides Vettakka, Jews also had estates in Chellanam, Mulavukadu, Maruvakadu and other islands around Cochin.

(Pearly Simon is the daughter-in-law of Paradesi Jewish leader A. I. Simon, who had an ongoing battle with Salem for years. Simon's grand-daughter Glennis Salem nee Simon, married Salem's grandson Leslie.)

"Hearing the commotion, Salem came out of his house and approached the agitators. He caught a couple of their leaders by their shirt collars and said: 'Today, it is Shabbat here. We want peace, so go and make this noise somewhere else,' and pushed them away from the gates of the homes. The agitators heard him without much argument and dispersed quickly because of his stature at that time among the working class of Mattancherry and Ernakulam."

Pearly Simon also remembers the grand Open House held by the Salem family every Simchat Torah and "I clearly recall how we all, adults and children, gathered at his house for a sumptuous meal. The children had stacks of sandwiches of different kinds and sweets and we all sat on huge carpets spread around the hall and ate and sang songs late into the night. A highlight of the meal was the ice-cream, which was a rare treat in Cochin at that time. The adults had their own party going in other sections of the house."[23]

And during Purim, Salem used to distribute newly minted coins that he brought specially from the bank to children of every house in Jew Town.

Pearly Simon describes Salem as 'an incredibly clever man, who just knew everything. People were in awe of him when he spoke and he had a wonderful mastery of English, Malayalam and Hebrew. He could have easily become the Diwan of Cochin if he had set his mind on it. But he squandered all his energy on the synagogue. Salem was a very active participant in the synagogue. He had a great singing voice and listeners would be spellbound with

23 Pearly Simon - Personal communication.

the tone and pitch and the intonations when he was praying or reading from the Torah.

"Despite what people said later, he was very friendly with Samuel Koder and Satu Koder. Salem's problem was that he was not consistent with anything."

Ruth Salem was also not much of a synagogue goer, according to Pearly. "She used to come on High Holidays or other celebrations - but generally kept away from synagogue life. She was attached to the Mattancherry Hospital - near the Boat Jetty, a little distance from the Pazhayanur temple entrance road and the Treasury. She helped deliver several hundred children throughout Cochin, including my daughter Glennis.'

"I remember Ruth, my mother Miriam Koder and other women getting together in the evening to sit outside the houses and talk about the day's events, family and world affairs."

Whenever Salem visited the Simon residence - Mandalay Hall - he usually took his own food with him. Pearly Simon says, "He had a particular way of eating... his wife Ruth used to prepare a plate with several small portions of a variety of colourful dishes... he was a diabetic and he stuck to a special eating ritual."

•••••

Salem suffered a stroke in 1959, after which he was confined to his wheelchair, bringing all his political activities to an end. He also stopped writing in his diary, a practice which he diligently followed for more than 45 years.

Salem died on April 20, 1967, just four days before his 85th birthday. He was buried near one of the walls of the Paradesi cemetery. Alongside are four other graves - of Ruth Salem and Raymond Salem on the right with Gumliel Salem and Reema Salem on the left.

BIBLIOGRAPHY

Barmouth, Eliyahu. *The Jews of Cochin: In Search of Roots*, Jerusalem, 2001.

Chiriyankandath, James. Nationalism, religion and community: A. B. Salem, the politics of identity and the disappearance of Cochin Jewry, *Journal of Global History* (2008). London School of Economics and Political Science 2008.

Cowen, Ida. *Jews in Remote Corners of the World*, Prentice-Hall, Englewood Cliffs, New Jersey, 1971.

Daniel, Ruby & Johnson, Barbara C. *Ruby of Cochin: An Indian Jewish Woman Remembers*, Jewish Publication Society, Philadelphia, 1995.

Forbes, James and Montalembert, Eliza Rosée. *Oriental Memoirs*, Richard Bentley, London, 1834.

Hamilton, Captain Alexander. *A New Account of the Indies*, London, C. Hitch and A. Millar, MDCCXLIV (1744).

Harris, Isidore Rev. Ed. *The Jewish Yearbook - Colonial Synagogues And Institutions*. London, 1907.

Johnson, Barbara. *Our Community in Two Worlds, The Cochin Paradesi Jews in India and Israel*, Ph.D theses, University of Massachusetts, 1985.

Jussay, P. M. *The Jews of Kerala*, University of Calicut, Kozhikode, 2005.

Katz, Nathan & Goldberg Ellen. *The Last Jews of Cochin: Jewish Identity in Hindu India*, University of South Carolina Press, 1993.

- Katz and Goldberg. The Sephardi Diaspora in Cochin, *Jewish*

Political Studies Review 5:3-4 (Fall 1993)

- Katz and Goldberg. Jewish "Apartheid" and a Jewish Gandhi, *Jewish Social Studies, Vol. 50, No. 3/4 (Summer, 1988 - Autumn, 1993).*

Kerala Government Archives. *Cochin Assembly Council proceedings, 1925-1945,* Trivandrum.

Kushner, Gilbert. *Immigrants from India in Israel: Planned change in an administered community,* University of Arizona Press, Tucson, 1973.

Lowell Thomas. *India: Land of the Black Pagoda,* P. F. Collier & Son Corp., New York, 1930.

Mandelbaum, David. The Jewish Way of Life in Cochin, *Jewish Social Studies, Vol. 1, No. 4* (Oct., 1939), pgs. 423-460 Published by: Indiana University Press Stable URL: http://www.jstor.org/stable/4464305.

Magnes Collection, *Global India: Kerala, Israel, Berkeley Case Study No. 4, Catalogue,* December 2013, University of California, Berkeley.

Menon, A. Sreedhara. *A Survey of Kerala History,* D.C. Books, Kottayam, Kerala, 2008.

Narayan T. C. *Ettu Kettu Stories,* Unison Publications, Bangalore, 2007.

Narayanan, M.G.S., *Cultural Symbiosis in Kerala,* Kerala Historical Society, Trivandrum, 1972.

Rabinowitz, Louis. *Far East Mission,* Eagle Press Limited. Johannesburg, 1952.

Sabharwal, Rohan. Film: *Where the Heart is. Jerusalem, Byzantium and then...Ernakulam,* 2013.

Salem, A. B. *Eternal Light or The Cochin Synagogue,* Ernakulam, 1929.

Segal, J. B. *A History of the The Jews of Cochin,* Valentine Mitchell, London, 1993.

Singh, Maina Chawla. *Being Indian, Being Israeli: Migration, Ethnicity and Gender in the Jewish Homeland,* Manohar Publishers, New Delhi, 2009.

Sreekala, S. *Israel's policy of "absorption of immigrants": a case study of the Indian Jews,* Jawaharlal Nehru University, 2000.

Wolff, Joseph Rev. *Travels and Adventures,* Saunders, Otley and Co., London, 1861.

9 780993 819933